Hebrews

by Leonard T. Wolcott

Copyright © 1988 by Graded Press

General Editor, Lynne M. Deming
Assistant Editor, Margaret Rogers
Copy Processing, Sylvia Marlow
Cover Design by Harriet Bateman

Scripture quotations in this publication, unless otherwise indicated, are from the Revised Standard Version of the Bible, copyrighted 1946, 1952, © 1971, 1973 by the Division of Christian Education of the National Council of the Churches of Christ in the U.S.A., and used by permission.

Maps in this publication are from the Oxford Bible Atlas edited by John May, 1984 (Third Edition), © Oxford University Press.

ISBN 0-939697-35-1

Table of Contents

Outline of Hebrews 4
Introduction to Hebrews 7
1. Hebrews 1 13
2. Hebrews 2 21
3. Hebrews 3:7–4:13 33
4. Hebrews 4:14–5:10 45
5. Hebrews 5:11–6:8 53
6. Hebrews 6:9-20 62
7. Hebrews 7 70
8. Hebrews 8:1–9:14 81
9. Hebrews 9:15–10:18 90
10. Hebrews 10:19-39 99
11. Hebrews 11:1-22 108
12. Hebrews 11:23-40 117
13. Hebrews 12:1-17 126
14. Hebrews 12:18-29 135
15. Hebrews 13 141
Glossary of Terms 151
Guide to Pronunciation 158
Map of Palestine 159

Outline of Hebrews

I. God Speaks Through Christ (1:1–3:6)
   A. God's nature is in the Son (1:1-14)
      1. God speaks to us through a Son (1:1-2)
      2. The Son's nature reflects God (1:3-4)
      3. The Son is superior to angels (1:5-7)
      4. God anointed the Son above all (1:8-9)
      5. The Son is before and beyond creation (1:10-12)
      6. The Son sits at God's right hand (1:13-14)
   B. Jesus made salvation possible (2:1–3:6)
      1. We dare not neglect salvation (2:1-2)
      2. Salvation was made known to us (2:3-4)
      3. The Lord suffered and died for us (2:5-9)
      4. Jesus identified with us (2:10-11)
      5. Jesus witnessed to us (2:12-13)
      6. Jesus' incarnation saves us (2:14-18)
      7. Consider the faithfulness of Jesus (3:1-2)
      8. Jesus is superior to Moses (3:2-6)

II. God Offers Access Through Christ (3:7–5:10)
   A. Do not reject Christ (3:7–4:13)
      1. Israel spoiled its chance (3:7-11)
      2. Let us not spoil our chance (3:12-15)
      3. The people missed God's rest (3:16-19)
      4. God's rest is still available (4:1-2)
      5. God's eternal sabbath rest (4:3-5)
      6. The opportunity remains (4:6-7)
      7. God's rest is greater (4:8-10)
      8. Strive to enter God's rest (4:11)
      9. The word of God knows us (4:12-13)
   B. Jesus is the perfect high priest (4:14–5:10)
      1. In faith draw near to God (4:14-16)
      2. High priests are appointed (5:1-4)
      3. God appointed Christ high priest (5:5-6)
      4. Jesus is our perfect high priest (5:7-10)

III. Grow Up in Faith and Press On (5:11–6:20)
   A. Grow up in your faith (5:11–6:8)
      1. You should be mature (5:11-14)
      2. Let us go on to maturity (6:1-3)
      3. You cannot begin again (6:4-6)
      4. Land produces good crops or weeds (6:7-8)
   B. Be confident in God's promise (6:9-20)
      1. You have done well (6:9-10)
      2. Imitate people of faith (6:11-12)
      3. God's promise to Abraham was sure (6:13-15)
      4. God's purpose is doubly sure (6:16-18)
      5. We can be confident (6:18-20)
IV. Christ Is High Priest for Our Salvation (7:1–10:39)
   A. Christ is supreme (7:1-28)
      1. Who is Melchizedek? (7:1-3)
      2. Melchizedek superior to old priesthood (7:4-10)
      3. The Levite priests were inadequate (7:11-12)
      4. There is a better order of priesthood (7:13-17)
      5. A greater hope supersedes the law (7:18-19)
      6. Christ is priest of a better covenant (7:20-22)
      7. Christ is our eternal high priest (7:23-25)
      8. Christ's sacrifice is permanent (7:26-28)
   B. A new covenant (8:1–9:14)
      1. High priest in the true sanctuary (8:1-2)
      2. Jesus is not in an earthly sanctuary (8:3-5)
      3. High priest of a better covenant (8:6-13)
      4. The first covenant had earthly rules (9:1-5)
      5. Rituals of the earthly sanctuary (9:6-10)
      6. Jesus, the one effective sacrifice (9:11-14)
   C. Christ's sacrifice purifies us (9:15–10:18)
      1. The new covenant becomes effective (9:15-17)
      2. Old covenant sealed by blood sacrifice (9:18-22)
      3. Christ mediates the new covenant (9:23-26)
      4. Jesus receives those who repent (9:27-28)
      5. Old sacrifices were repeated (10:1-4)
      6. Christ replaced the old sacrifices (10:5-10)
      7. Christ has purified his people (10:11-14)
      8. The new covenant of God's grace (10:15-18)

- D. Persevere in Christ (10:19-39)
    1. Jesus has opened the way to God (10:19-21)
    2. Let us draw near with faith (10:22-23)
    3. Let us encourage one another (10:24-25)
    4. Do not spurn Christ's sacrifice (10:26-31)
    5. Recall faith experiences (10:32-34)
    6. Persevere with confidence (10:35-39)
- V. Live the Life of Faith (11:1–12:29)
    - A. Imitate examples of faith (11:1-40)
        1. Faith is confidence in the expected (11:1-3)
        2. By faith Abel and Enoch pleased God (11:4-6)
        3. Noah: heir of righteousness (11:7)
        4. Abraham went out in faith (11:8-10)
        5. Sarah trusted God's promise (11:11-12)
        6. Confidence in things hoped for (11:13-16)
        7. Abraham and Isaac (11:17-19)
        8. Isaac, Jacob, and Joseph trusted God (11:20-22)
        9. Moses lived by faith (11:23-28)
        10. Israel came to Canaan by faith (11:29-31)
        11. Strong leaders and prophets (11:32-34)
        12. Faith in times of suffering (11:35-38)
        13. Faith in God's promise (11:39-40)
    - B. Persevere through hardship (12:1-17)
        1. Follow Jesus in faith (12:1-2)
        2. Persevere through suffering (12:3-6)
        3. Discipline leads to righteousness (12:7-11)
        4. Therefore, be strong (12:12-13)
        5. Live in peace and goodness (12:14-17)
    - C. Come to the joyful city of God (12:18-29)
        1. Yours is not a religion of fear (12:18-21)
        2. Come to the joyful city of God (12:22-24)
        3. Do not refuse God who calls you (12:25-27)
        4. Worship God with thankfulness (12:28-29)
- VI. In Conclusion (13:1-25)
    - A. Be faithful fellow Christians (13:1-17)
    - B. Closing of the letter (13:18-21)
    - C. Postscript (13:22-25)

Introduction to Hebrews

Hebrews is unique in the New Testament. It has the richest vocabulary, the most eloquent Greek, yet the style of the Jewish rabbis. It quotes the Old Testament most frequently and at greatest length. It has the severest warning and the warmest encouragement for Christians to be faithful.

Hebrews is about Jesus Christ, what he has done and what he is. It is a message of hope, a promise of eternal fellowship with God, conditioned only on our response. It is about God's awesome greatness, perfect righteousness, and grace and love inviting us to respond. Hebrews is a book of action, of persevering movement toward God, into God's presence.

Authorship

Who wrote the letter? We do not know. Shortly after it was written, no one knew. People guessed. We are still guessing.

Some have guessed that Paul wrote the letter. Saying Paul wrote it helped to get Hebrews accepted when Christians were deciding what to include in the New Testament. It was not written by Paul, however. The style, vocabulary, and emphases are not Paul's. Others have guessed it was Barnabas because he encouraged people (Acts 4:36) as Hebrews does. Some have guessed Priscilla because she and her husband, Aquila, instructed a man named Apollos in the gospel (Acts 18:26). Many have guessed Apollos himself, *an eloquent man, well versed in Scripture* (Acts 18:24), and a leading preacher (1 Corinthians 1:12).

Proof of authorship is not needed to appreciate the value of what has been written. Whoever wrote the letter to the Hebrews was gifted in speech, as well as in vocabulary and style. This anonymous writer knew his contemporary culture and literature. He knew how Jewish rabbis taught. Greek was the universal language of the time, and he knew how Greek authors wrote. From Jewish Scriptures (the Old Testament) he drew symbols and illustrations to press home a message of warning and encouragement for the Christians of his day.

The Audience

To whom was the message sent? Where did they live? We do not know. Again, there have been many guesses such as somewhere in Italy, in Judea, in Egypt. Someone added on the title "To the Hebrews" because the author refers extensively to Hebrew stories and worship in the Old Testament.

All Christians, however, whether of Jewish or pagan background, were accustomed to "search the Scriptures," that is, the Old Testament, to read what it said about the Messiah, Christ. All we know is that the letter was addressed to Christians who needed encouragement. It tells us that they were at one time new and joyful Christians. They have had troubles, however, maybe ridicule or persecution that has disheartened them. They have become lax in the practice of their faith.

Date

When was Hebrews written? A Christian in about A.D. 90 wrote a letter from Rome in which he quoted from Hebrews. About the same time it was being quoted in Alexandria, Egypt. So we know it was written by A.D. 90. How long before? We do not know, except that Timothy, evidently the Apostle Paul's young friend, was still active (13:23).

Literary Style

Was Hebrews a letter? We do not know even that. It begins with no greetings, no address, and has no signature. The last chapter reads like the closing of a letter from a Christian leader with words of counsel, a benediction, a postscript with news about coming with Timothy, and with the phrase *Grace be with all of you.*

The previous parts (twelve chapters in our Bible) read like a lecture or sermon. Was it a sermon—or several short sermons—which someone sent to a group of Christians, attaching a personal note? Was it a tract? In this commentary it will frequently be referred to as a sermon.

One thing we do know. Hebrews is a masterpiece, a beautiful and intense expression of faith and hope applicable to all Christians.

The Theme of Hebrews

There is a triple theme in Hebrews: (1) movement from the inadequate to the adequate, from the imperfect to the perfect, to God; (2) Christ who alone is supremely sufficient to make that movement possible; and (3) warning and encouragement to persevere in that Christ-enabled movement.

The Logic of Hebrews

(1) The assumption is that the business of life, and the desire of all people, is access to God. Everlasting separation from God is the ultimate tragedy.

(2) The problem is that sin and indifferent neglect of faith prevent fellowship with God.

(3) The need is to break through sin's wall of separation.

(4) The solution is Christ. Through Christ we can be forgiven. Through Christ we gain access to God.

(5) The responsibility is ours to accept forgiveness, and to move toward communion with God through faithfulness to Christ who opens up the way.

The Message of Hebrews

Hebrews is a warning against the neglect of what God has offered in Christ. Rejecting Christ means rejecting God, God's Word, God's Spirit, God's grace. It is a warning against drifting off into the inadequacies of pre-Christian Judaism, or into exotic cults or into immorality, or into mere indifference and neglect. But Hebrews is also an encouragement to endure suffering, to persevere in faithfulness to Christ. It is an assurance that God's promise is unfailing, and that Christ is the supreme and only adequate means of our inheriting that promise. That promise is salvation, purification, perfection, "rest" in God's presence forever.

The warnings and encouragement interweave with illustrations and arguments that point out Christ's superiority as God's one appointed means of salvation.

Christ in Hebrews Is Our High Priest

Hebrews calls Christ a high priest because, like a priest, he offers a sacrifice on behalf of people. Hebrews uses a story from Genesis (14:17-20) to illustrate Christ's high priesthood. Melchizedek was a priest-king who blessed Abraham, ancestor of the Israelites. Melchizedek was not an Israelite. The story mentions no lineage, birth, or death of Melchizedek. Christ, says Hebrews, is like that (6:20). Using contrast, Hebrews points out the superiority of Christ as the only effective priest for our salvation (7:11, 16, 22; 9:13-14, 23).

The Old Testament in Hebrews

When people became Christians, they inherited the Jewish faith based on the Jewish interpretation of the Old Testament at the time of Jesus. Christians studied the Old Testament and knew it well. The Hebrews sermon shows how Jesus fulfilled the religious hope and faith of the Old Testament. Here are the main elements of Jewish-biblical faith emphasized in Hebrews.

(1) Stories of the Jews' ancestors are about people of

faith in God's righteousness.

(2) God called Abraham and promised him and his descendants a great posterity (Genesis 12–50).

(3) Abraham was met and blessed by Melchizedek, a king-priest (Genesis 14:17-20).

(4) Abraham's descendants, the people of Israel, traveled through the Sinai desert country as refugees from Egypt seeking a better country. Led by Moses, they were assured of God's guidance and help. Nevertheless, they complained (Exodus 15:22-25; 17:1-7; Numbers 14; Psalm 95:7-11).

(5) God made a covenant with the people of Israel, promising to bring them to a land of rest, and giving them a law to live by. The people promised to obey the law. Moses, their leader, confirmed the covenant by sacrificing oxen and sprinkling the blood on the people (Exodus 24:7-8).

(6) Moses constructed a tent of meeting on the pattern God gave him (Exodus 25:8-9; 40:1-11, 16-33). This tent of meeting became the sanctuary where the people gathered to worship God. (See chart and description of the tent of meeting on page 159.)

(7) Aaron, brother of Moses, was appointed high priest of the sanctuary. Their tribe, the Levites, was set aside to assist the priests, Aaron's descendants, who conducted religious ceremonies as representatives of the people before God (Exodus 40:12-15).

(8) The ceremonies of worship at the tent of meeting included sacrifices of animals, ritually killed. Their blood, the essence of the sacrificed life, was sprinkled as a symbolic cleansing.

(9) The most important ceremony took place once a year on the Day of Atonement. On this day only, the high priest entered the Most Holy Place of the tent of meeting carrying the blood of the sacrificed animals which he sprinkled on the mercy seat (the cover of the box called the ark of the covenant). The mercy seat represented God's presence. The high priest stood before

God as a mediator asking God to forgive the people their sins. By this ritual, the sins God's people had committed during the year were said to be forgiven so that their covenant with God might continue (Leviticus 16). This ceremony had to be repeated each year. It was preceded by a sin offering to cover the sins of the high priest before he could enter the Most Holy Place. Sin offerings were also made for the sins of the priests.

(10) After the death of Moses, Joshua led the people of Israel into Canaan, the promised land of rest (Joshua 1:1-4).

(11) Much later, when the Jewish nation was conquered and many were taken into exile, there developed the hope for a great "Day of the Lord." It would be at the end of time when God would destroy Israel's enemies. The people of earth would unite in worship of God, and righteousness would prevail in the earth.

PART ONE Hebrews 1

Introduction to This Chapter

God speaks to us through *a Son*. The message of Hebrews begins with this fundamental declaration: Through a son God has made the final revelation, completing all the partial revelations of the past. The author quotes Scripture to assure his readers about the ultimate and supreme significance of the Son through whom God discloses the divine mind and purpose.

Here is an outline of Chapter 1.
I. God Speaks to Us Through a Son (1:1-2)
II. The Son's Nature Reflects God (1:3-4)
III. The Son Is Superior to Angels (1:5-7)
IV. God Anointed the Son Above All (1:8-9)
V. The Son Is Before and Beyond Creation (1:10-12)
VI. The Son Sits at God's Right Hand (1:13-14)

God Speaks to Us Through a Son (1:1-2)

Verses 1 through 4 are the author's theme which the whole sermon develops about Christ. Like the first verse of the Gospel of John, the first phrase in Hebrews is about God's word. With a literary flourish—*In many and various ways*—it tells how God communicated through interpreters, the prophets. *Prophets* is used loosely of all those in the Old Testament who responded to God's purpose. In those ancient times God was revealed bit by bit, little by little. Just as children learn little by little, the people were unable to grasp all learning at once. There is a sense of marvelous contrast here. Those past revelations were good and richly varied, but fragmentary. They were to the *fathers*. All persons of faith in God were spiritual ancestors of Christians of both Jewish and non-Jewish descent (as in 1 Corinthians 10:1). *But now* . . . we, the spiritual descendants of the ancient Hebrews, are receiving the final full revelation. . . . *in these last days* . . . . Our times, the writer is saying, are the last days, a phrase used in the Old Testament for the hoped-for days of fulfillment (Isaiah 2:2). First-century Christians were sure that they were living in the time of consummation of the ages which would quickly come to a climax with the return of Christ. It is the essential quality of New Testament faith: that we live in, and by, the "end times." God is in the process of fulfilling the divine purpose through *a Son* who is both heir and instrument of all creation. The Son who creates is also the Son who communicates to us God's redeeming forgiveness, as the Hebrews sermon will go on to point out.

Here Hebrews starts a pattern, used throughout the letter, of contrast between the old and the new. The movement is always away from the old, which is insufficient, to the new, which is all-sufficient.

A Son, who he is and what makes him so extremely significant, is what the letter sets out to explain. The word *Son* itself signifies a relationship. He is nearer to God than were the prophets or, as to be indicated later, the angels. This *Son* is also related to humanity. He is the bridge of communication between God and humankind. *The world* is plural in the Greek, and signifies the universe, not just our world or our time. God created the world—the universe or "the ages"—through the Son who was appointed its heir. The word *heir*, like *Son*, also signifies a relationship which neither prophets nor angels have to God. Since God is eternal, the eternalness of the heir is implied. The Son was not *created* but *creative*. Jewish thinkers, particularly those influenced by the university center at Alexandria in Egypt, had long been writing about the *wisdom* or the *word* of God through which God had from the beginning created the universe and expressed the divine nature (Proverbs 8:22-31). Hebrews, like John's Gospel (John 1:1-3) and Paul (Colossians 1:15-17), identifies *wisdom* and *word* with Christ. This statement, joined with *upholding the universe* and *made purification for sins* (verse 3), identifies Christ's creative power with his redemptive function. Through him we have our creation and through him we receive our redemption from sin. (See 1 Corinthians 8:6.)

The Son's Nature Reflects God (1:3-4)

The phrase *son of* in Hebrew idiom was used of a person who was like, similar to, or had the nature of what or whomever he was a *son of*. *The Son* the author of Hebrews writes about *reflects the glory of God*. Think of God as a glowing, brilliant, everlasting light. The Son is the radiance of that light (John 1:4-5). The Son is one who *bears the very stamp of his* [God's] *nature*. The stamp was the same as a seal. A seal, pressed to a manuscript, left its image. The Son is engraved with the nature of God. If you have not seen a person, but have seen an exact statue or photograph of that person, you know what he or she looks like. The Son duplicates for us the nature of God, because of his close association with God. As John's Gospel describes it: *The Word was with God, and the Word was God* (John 1:1).

Hebrews speaks of the Son as *upholding the universe by his word of power* [powerful word]. That is like Paul's statement that *in him* [the Son] *all things hold together* (Colossians 1:17). *Word*, in Hebrews, sometimes has the sense of a *decree* by God or Christ. His decree of creative authority bears up the universe.

God acts through the Son's acts. The Son made *purification for sins* and *sat at the right hand of* God. Much of Hebrews' message centers on these two acts of Christ. *When he had made purification for sins, he sat down . . . .*

This key phrase centers on what the Son did and does for us. This is the basis for the letter's appeal for our faith in and faithfulness to Christ.

Purification is a priestly act. By interceding for and making sacrifice for the worshiper, the priest purifies the worshiper. Purification and salvation and perfection in this sermon all have to do with being made presentable to God. God's revelation through a Son is not simply a reference to Jesus' life and teachings, but to Christ's crucifixion, resurrection, and perpetual presence before God as our high priest, where he cleanses us from our sins that have kept us from God.

. . . *He sat down at the right hand* of God. This phrase indicates the completion of the Son's priestly sacrifice. The imagery is that of God as a king. None but royalty may sit in the king's presence. His *right hand* indicates a position of honor and authority.

The Son Is Superior to Angels (1:5-7)

Verses 5 through 14 are the first lesson of the sermon: the superiority of Christ over the angels. Jews at that time accepted the idea of angels as servants of God, carrying out God's commands. Some thinkers, called *gnostics*, even taught that angels issued directly from God. Hebrews uses biblical passages to prove that this cannot be so. Angels are created, and the creative Christ is superior to them. To Hebrews, all Scripture (our Old Testament) is God's word. Therefore, passages from Scripture are direct quotations from God (or from Christ, or the Spirit). The first quotation (verse 5) is from Psalm 2:7. This was an oracle addressed to the king, a descendant of the dynasty of David, on his enthronement. At the time Hebrews was written, the psalm was understood to be a reference to the messiah, as in Acts 13:33. The messiah would come someday as a divinely appointed hero to save and reign over his people, Israel. Like a king, he would be anointed with oil, but specially anointed by God. Most Jews were eagerly expecting him. Psalm 2:7 is here applied to the messiah's consecration by God. *Christ* is the Greek translation of *messiah, the anointed one*. The writer probably knew about the voice from heaven at Jesus' baptism: *Thou art my beloved son* (Mark 1:11).

The next quotation, *I will be to him a father* . . . , is from 2 Samuel 7:14 and 1 Chronicles 17:13. This passage was also considered to apply to the messiah. God is called *Father of spirits* in 12:9. Otherwise, Hebrews does not speak of God as *Father*.

The *first-born* in verse 6 is a reference to the Son's priority with God. As Paul says, *He is before all things . . . the first-born* (Colossians 1:17-18). The meaning of *when* is not clear.

God's statement to the angels is drawn from a passage in the old Greek translation of the Song of Moses (Deuteronomy 32). There *worship* was literally *prostrate yourselves*, as an inferior would do only before one who was greatly superior.

If we compare the next quotation, verse 7, with its source, Psalm 104:4, we can see how the author's Greek translation placed the objects in inverted form from the way we read it in English. In the old Greek, *angels* (messengers) are made into *winds*, *servants* (ministers) into *fire*. Rabbis of the author's day believed this happened to angels. Like winds or fire, they might die down. But the Son, says Hebrews, never dies, never changes.

God Anointed the Son Above All (1:8-9)

Infrequently in Jewish literature, angels had been referred to as *sons* (never *a son*) of God. The writer makes the distinction clear. There is only one Son. To sharpen the contrast, the writer uses Psalm 45:6-7. This psalm was originally a love song celebrating the marriage of the king. Hebrews quotes it from the old Greek text as God's address to the king: *Your throne, O God, is forever*.

The Son, in many translations, seems to be addressed as God, as though God were calling the Son God, saying, in verse 9, that he, God, has anointed God, the Son. In one other New Testament passage, Jesus, as risen Lord, is addressed as *My Lord and my God* (John 20:28). The emphasis in Psalm 45:6, however, is that the throne is divine and forever. The Revised Standard Version translation of the psalm is, *Your divine throne endures forever*, with the alternate suggestion: *Your throne is a throne of God*. This is in line with the Hebrew concept that the anointing of the king is an imparting of the spirit from God. Earlier translations read *God is your throne* or *Your throne is God*. These translations correspond to other statements in Hebrews that Christ completed his career by being enthroned in heaven at the right hand of God.

A *scepter* is the symbol of the king's rule as head of government (verse 8). *Righteousness* is willing and doing that which is consistent with the nature of God who is just and right. In Hebrews, as in all the New Testament, righteousness includes God's anger against sin, at wrongdoing. At the same time, it is Christ's suffering love for sinners, making possible their salvation.

At his coronation, the king was anointed with oil (verse 9). This symbolized the transmission to the king of a portion of God's spirit and holiness (see 1 Samuel 16:13). *Messiah* (the Hebrew word for *Christ*) means *the anointed one*. The fact that God so honors the Son is an important point which the sermon takes up later (2:9). He is anointed *beyond thy comrades*, above his fellows. Of no angel can this be said. The anointing is with the *oil of gladness* in joyful celebration. He is exalted because he has done what is right to God and people, and has resisted what is wrong.

The Son Is Before and Beyond Creation (1:10-12)

Hebrews moves on to Psalm 102:26-28. What this psalm of hope says about God's creative action, Hebrews uses to express the Son's creative action. God and Son are not identified as the same, however. God addresses the son who has been appointed and through whom God creates (verse 2) and whom God anointed (verse 9). The angels were only spectators at the creation (see Job 38:7, where *sons of God* is translated as *angels* in the Greek Bible used by Hebrews). The creative Son is superior over all that is created (verses 11-12). The created universe will serve its purpose for awhile, but in time it will wear out. The picturesque language sees the skies, which wrap the earth, rolled up like a worn out mantle that wraps the body. This accentuates the emphasis on the unchanging nature of the Son. *But thou art the same* (see 13:8).

The Son Sits at God's Right Hand (1:13-14)

The major text for Hebrews' explanation of Christ will be Psalm 110. Here the writer quotes the first verse of the psalm. This was a popular verse used by early Christians to express Christ (see verse 3, above). God gives this honor only to the Son. In contrast, the angels, all of them, are simply *ministering spirits*, servants of the one who sits on the throne, sent forth to serve, to carry out God's good plan for the people and to help them. There is a distinction intended here between angels who serve as commissioned by God, on God's initiative, not theirs, and the Son who is a partner in God's initiative. The ministering function of angels appears in many biblical narratives. In this passage their commission is to serve God's main purpose, which is effected through the Son, the saving of humankind. *Those who are to obtain salvation* in a more literal translation is, *those who are about to inherit salvation*. Salvation, the ultimate wholeness in community with Christ and God, is what Christians look forward to. It is God's promise about to be realized by those who accept it. That is what makes faithfulness to Christ, according to Hebrews, a religion of joyous expectancy. (Hebrews explains salvation in 2:9-18; 5:8-9.)

§ § § § § § §

The Message of Hebrews 1

God's revelation has come in many ways, but the fullest revelation comes through Christ.

The Christian faith is Christ. It is not a system of belief woven about Christ, but Christ himself. In order to warn and encourage Christians concerning their faith in and faithfulness to Christ, the letter to the Hebrews must make clear who and what Christ is, what he has done, does, and will do, and why he is so very important.

To begin with, Christ is, in relation to God, *a Son. A Son* implies a priority in relationship, a pre-eminence that can be superceded by no one and by no thing. The Son reflects God and shares *God's word of power*. Christ is also related to us, as God's message to us for our redemption.

Chapter 1 of Hebrews tells us about the Son, that:

§ He was appointed and anointed by God.

§ He was God's instrument in creating the universe.

§ He made it possible for us to be purified from sin and that, having done so, he remains in the presence of God.

§ As Creator he is superior to all created things; and, although all things decay, he endures forever.

Chapter 1 of Hebrews is like a doorway from the old to the new, from former times when people had only glimpses of God to a full awareness of what God is and what God does and has for us. This chapter prepares us to understand the full message of Hebrews, that:

§ The goal of history is about to be realized.

§ The promises of God are about to be fulfilled.

§ The purpose of life is about to be consummated in the experience of salvation.

§ And all this is made possible through Jesus Christ for those who are faithful to him.

§ § § § § § §

PART TWO Hebrews 2

Introduction to This Chapter

Having stressed the significance of the Son as the medium of salvation, Hebrews warns readers against neglecting that salvation. It is such a grand offer, attested by God. The sermon then explains how Jesus, the glorified Son, identified with and suffered for people in order to free them from sin.

In order to encourage Christian faithfulness, the writer to the Hebrews has affirmed the superiority of Jesus, the Son, over angels. He was given charge of the universe and appointed by God to be high priest representing the people. Through his incarnation and suffering death, Jesus has atoned for the sins of the people.

Nevertheless, there were many who were inclined to give greater attention to Moses, to whom God gave the holy law and covenant, and to Joshua, the hero, who led God's people into the Promised Land. Therefore, the writer sets out to explain how Jesus goes farther than the law and brings people to a truer goal, and is, therefore, much greater than Moses and Joshua. It is through Jesus only, Hebrews says, that people can arrive at the place of rest God intended for them.

Here is an outline of Hebrews 2:1–3:6.
  I. We Dare Not Neglect Salvation (2:1-2)
  II. Salvation Was Made Known to Us (2:3-4)
  III. The Lord Suffered and Died for Us (2:5-9)
  IV. Jesus Identified With Us (2:10-11)
  V. Jesus Witnessed to Us (2:12-13)

   VI. Jesus' Incarnation Saves Us (2:14-18)
  VII. Consider the Faithfulness of Jesus (3:1-2)
 VIII. Jesus Is Superior to Moses (3:2-6)

We Dare Not Neglect Salvation (2:1-2)

Verses 1-4 include the first urgent counsel of the sermon. In these counsels, the author alternates between *we* and *you*, between identifying with the hearers and addressing them as a teacher would.

The theme of Chapter 1 was Christ. The last word in that chapter is *salvation*. This is the key word for Chapter 2. Our salvation lies in what Christ has done for us. The offer of salvation is universal and includes both the preacher and the audience. It applies to all. What we have heard is the reality of the gospel.

Lest we drift away, like a boat gliding aimlessly past its dock to be washed away by the tide: This is a picture of sin that means, literally, missing the mark, or, in this illustration, letting our lives slip away from the truth.

Here is the sermon's first contrast between the good and the better. A popular idea was that angels brought the law of God to Moses on Mount Sinai. The law they brought was good, *valid*. The writer, like the readers of the sermon, had confidence in the reliability of the law because it was a part of the word of God as found in their Bible (Old Testament). Accordingly, the writer uses the word *message*, which could also be translated as *word*, rather than simply as *law declared by angels*. Every *transgression* (deviation from the law), or *disobedience* (failure to heed the law), flouting its orders, was bad, and brought on, inevitably, punishment. *Retribution* means *payment of wages*. Faithfulness brought the good wages of reward (11:26). Faithlessness deserved the bad wages of punishment.

God's great gift of the truth, the gospel brought by the Son, is greater than the law. Therefore, to neglect it, to disregard or slight it, is worse than violating the law. So great an opportunity for life, for eternity, and we fail to have any interest in it? The consequence is immeasurable loss. This is the tragedy of a life lived in indifference to the gospel. It lets an exceptional opportunity for salvation slip away.

Obeying the law was a means of pleasing God, but the salvation offered by the Son is more effective than the law, because it enables those who receive it to draw near to God. The reward is God's presence. The punishment for neglecting it is missing God in life and eternity.

Salvation Was Made Known to Us (2:3-4)

We do not have the excuse of ignorance about this great offer of salvation, because it was made known to us. First of all, *the Lord* (Jesus) declared it by what he was, by what he did among the people, suffering to bring them salvation. Second, those who heard Jesus and saw him in ministry *attested*, confirmed, what the Lord declared. *Attested* in Greek corresponds to the adjective *valid* in verse 2. Those who saw and heard and knew Jesus have assured us of the validity and trustworthiness of his message. Third, God added a corroborative witness by means of *signs* which aroused the amazed wonder of those who saw them. *Various miracles* were associated with the preaching of this salvation as evidences of God's power (see Mark 16:20). Paul had written that the *signs and wonders and mighty works* were signs of the true apostle (2 Corinthians 12:12). The Book of Acts tells miracle stories such as must have been familiar to the author of Hebrews. These signs were a foretaste of the *powers of the age to come* (6:5). The dynamic evidence of this salvation was God's gift of the Holy Spirit, which was distributed in a variety of abilities among believers. (Paul also wrote about *varieties of gifts, but the same Spirit* in 1 Corinthians 12:1-13.) These are distributed according to God's own will. They are not human devices. They are inspired by the Spirit, not organized by persons.

The Lord Suffered and Died for Us (2:5-9)

Now the author takes up the second lesson of the sermon, about the passion and ministry of Christ for us. The passage is difficult, but central to the sermon.

There had been criticisms: Jesus was human, so he could not have been as great as the angels, who were superhuman. Moreover, Jesus suffered and died. This has always remained a stumbling-block to many people. How could a divine one suffer and die at the hands of men? The writer quotes Psalm 8:4-6 to refute these arguments.

First, however, it must be made clear that God did not subject the world to come under angels. (The idea of subjection is taken from the psalm.) This is the first of several references in Hebrews to that which is to come, about to be: *the age to come* (6:5), *the good things to come* (10:1), *the city which is to come* (13:14). The author has in mind the consummation, the ultimate fulfillment when salvation will be fully realized (9:28). The word for *world* in this passage is the world of people *who are to obtain salvation* (1:14). As servants of God, angels can help them (1:14), but, as the psalm quoted declares, it is Christ who will reign over this new world. Christ, then, is more important than angels to Christians.

It has been testified, or affirmed. The author does not say, "God (Christ or Holy Spirit) says," but it is still in the author's mind that God said this somewhere. If the author quoted this from memory, it was an exact memory of the passage in the Greek Bible.

Psalm 8 was generally accepted as a psalm about the messiah. *Son of man* in the Hebrew psalm had simply been a parallel to *man* in the previous verse, that is, human being. By the time of Christ, however, the term *Son of man* had become a commonly accepted reference to the messiah to come. So the psalm, although phrased in the past tense, was taken as a prophecy about the messiah, the *Son of man*. Hebrews, like Paul, does not use this title for Jesus, yet has no problem with it as a reference to the messiah. According to this interpretation, the psalm says in one breath that this man (the messiah) was made a little lower than the angels, but also that he was *crowned with glory and honor*, everything *being put under his feet. Everything* included angels. It left nothing outside the messiah's control.

However, we do not see everything in subjection to him. Paul, discussing this same verse from Psalm 8 in 1 Corinthians 15:24-26, speaks of a period of successive subduing of his enemies by the reigning Christ at the end of time. The full subjection of all things under Christ has obviously not yet taken place. It will take place in the world to come. That will coincide with the full realization of our salvation we have yet to obtain (1:14; 9:28).

This gives the writer occasion to bring out the heart of the message about the connection of Jesus to salvation: Through his suffering death, Jesus made salvation possible. This is the salvation *declared at first by the Lord* (2:3) in his ministry, but especially by his agony in purging away the results of human sin. He was made *lower than the angels for a little while* (as Hebrews reads it, instead of *a little lower than the angels* as we read it in our English version). The *little while* was the period of his incarnation as a human being *in the days of his flesh* (5:7). It is the story of one who is eternal, the very creative force of the universe who ultimately becomes crowned with glory eternally at God's side. The interim, before the final crowning, is what Hebrews is concerned with now. It is because of what the Lord was and is that, for a short time, subject to all human limitations and temptations, he was able to take upon himself suffering and death in behalf of human beings. That gave him the power to clear the way through sin to salvation for all.

Here, for the first time, Hebrews calls the *Lord*, the *Son*, by his human name, *Jesus*. Jesus, the Hebrews sermon says, is made lower than the angels so that he might suffer death. Because of the suffering of death, in his incarnation, Jesus is crowned with glory and honor, conferred on him by God. It is the highest possible divine dignity and includes authority over all creation. The purpose of his suffering death was that he might taste death for everyone. No mere brush with death is meant by *taste*, but that he suffered the full agony of every human death. Angels could never do this, because as *ministering spirits* they could never become human and share and overcome the human predicament of sin.

His suffering death was not an indication of powerlessness in the face of human circumstances. Rather, it happened by God's grace. God, through Christ's suffering and death, was making an offer of salvation to people. Because death was considered a result of the sin of Adam, it was believed that, because of sin, people die. Jesus, the sinless one, died for the sins of others, absolving them of their sins.

Some commentators think Hebrews interprets Psalm 8 as a statement, not about the messiah, but about the human species in general: Humankind has been created to rule over nature. We have been made *lower than the angels for a little while*, although our destiny is to be exalted over the angels. This has not happened yet, because sin and suffering and death have enslaved human nature. There is hope, however. Jesus, Lord of creation, has taken upon himself this human role in order to deliver persons from their bonds and free them to become the exalted creatures God intended.

Jesus Identified With Us (2:10-11)

Jesus could be for us because he was with us, like us, fully human, while at the same time the unique instrument of God.

This passage can only make sense if *he*, in verse 10, refers to God. This makes clear that Christ is Creator (1:2, 10) only as an instrument of God, *for whom and by whom all things exist* (see Romans 11:36). Christ is also

Redeemer, *tasting death for everyone* (verse 9) as an agent for God who is the one who brings *many sons to glory*. *Sons* is, of course, here an inclusive term for *people*. It is parallel in the sentence to *Son* who, as Jesus, performs the action by which God brings people to salvation.

As before, the writer shows that the perfecting of Jesus came through his suffering. This emphasis gives suffering a radical new definition. In early tribal (and early Hebrew) culture, suffering could be the result of breaking "tabu." To the developed Hebrew thinking, it was the consequence of disobeying God's will. But here, suffering is essential in Jesus' obedience to God's will to make salvation possible for people. The Hebrews sermon will expand this thought in later passages.

Verses 11 through 13 stress the identification of Christ with people who accept the gift of salvation. This identification is necessary, as Hebrews will explain (verses 14, 17, 18), for Christ's suffering and death to be effective. No angel and no non-mortal god could be effective. They would be unrelated to human beings.

The illustration is from the religious sanctuary. To *sanctify* or *make holy* is a priestly function. The priest is, like those who come to him, a human being, whose ritual brings both himself and the attending worshipers before the holy presence of God. Christ, as incarnate Jesus, shares one human origin with all people.

Jesus Witnessed to Us (2:12-13)

Through his incarnation, his suffering, and his physical death, Jesus was able to witness to his fellow human beings and to present them to God.

Hebrews finds support for this thought in two Old Testament passages. In Psalm 22:22 the psalmist speaks of praising God among his fellow Israelites. Hebrews associates this praise with Jesus' praising God among his people. They are his *brothers*. That is, he is one with them, of the same human family.

Hebrews then quotes Isaiah 8:17-18. The prophet says he puts his trust in God. Christ, carrying out God's purpose through his incarnation, is dependent on God.

In the next verse (Isaiah 8:18), the prophet presents himself and his children as signs from the Lord. In his incarnation, Jesus gathers disciples and shares their lives as they do his. Because a teacher's disciples were sometimes spoken of as his "children" in Greek, the writer of Hebrews may have had this in mind when quoting this verse as proof of Jesus' community with human nature.

Jesus' Incarnation Saves Us (2:14-18)

Because Jesus shared humanity with people *in every respect* (verse 17), their experiences, their suffering, and even their temptations, he was able to overcome death and the devil and help people overcome their fear of death. As one of them, yet from God, he could mediate their sins, overcoming their sins for them.

No angel could do this. It was not with angels, however, that he was concerned, but with people of flesh and blood. The descendants of Abraham are Jews, but are also all believing Christians who have inherited the faith of Abraham (Hebrews 11).

In popular belief the devil was the angel of death, and people, by sinning, came under the power of death. Salvation, the essence of the full life, is liberation from death and from the life-long bondage of the fear of death.

Verse 17 summarizes what has been said to this point: God speaks to us through a Son who has been made like us. This verse also opens the discussion and explanation of the Son's function as a merciful and faithful high priest in the service of God. This will be developed in Chapters 5 through 10.

The chief function of Israel's high priest was his annual, once-a-year entry into the Most Holy Place in the sanctuary to make atonement for the sins of the people.

To make expiation for the sins of the people was to remove the barrier sin had built up between the people and God. Jesus now expiates their sins, removing the barrier between them and God.

He could not have done this if he had not had the human experience of temptation. Temptation gave him understanding of the power of sin to bar people from God. It gave him a sympathy with fellow human beings as he suffered in their behalf (Mark 10:45).

Consider the Faithfulness of Jesus (3:1-2)

The writer addresses the readers with a warm appeal. There are three words here which were generally used for fellow Christians: *holy, brothers,* and *called.* They were *holy* (the same word is often translated as a noun: *saints*), because they belonged to the Holy One, Jesus. They were set apart from other people in their dedication to Jesus. By accepting Jesus' sacrifice for them, they were *sanctified,* or *made holy* (2:11). They were *brothers,* the inclusive word meaning members of one family. They were called by God through Christ to be God's people. *Heaven* was used as a synonym for God with reference to God's eternal dwelling. Their *heavenly call* is a divine call to come to God. A fourth word is *sharer,* or *participant,* translated in the Revised Standard Version as *who share.* The calling is always a shared call.

Holiness is always a community experience of Christians. That community relationship has been established—as just explained in the previous passage—by Jesus in his incarnation. Therefore what Christ has done for us is the basis for the sermon's appeal to us. The first verse also prepares us to consider, in some later passages, Christ's apostleship and priesthood.

Apostle means *one sent,* an appointed representative who speaks for the one who sent him. Jesus is God's appointed. That is important in Hebrews. The appointed

Jesus is sent. Jesus also represents us before God as the high priest of our confession. Our confession centers in Jesus, the one whom we together accept as our high priest. In him we agree.

Jesus focuses our faith on God, to whom he is faithful. Jesus is faithful to God *who appointed him* to be *heir of all things* (1:2, 9) and to be *a faithful high priest* (2:17). The Hebrews sermon is a call to all Christians to be faithful.

Jesus Is Superior to Moses (3:2-6)

What about Moses? He, too, was faithful. He, too, was sent by God to Israel. He, too, frequently acted as a high priest, interceding for the people (see Exodus 32:11-14; Numbers 14:13-19). Christians, whether they are of Jewish background or not, inherited the Jewish Bible and the Jewish confidence in Moses. Moses had delivered the people of Israel from slavery in Egypt and had led them across the desert toward a Promised Land (compare 2:10). Moses was God's spokesman to Israel in the wilderness of Sinai (Exodus 32:11-14). Moses transmitted laws by which life could be measured and regulated. Moses was *faithful in God's house*: Hebrews has in mind Numbers 12:7 where God says of Moses, *He is entrusted with all my house.* The sanctuary Moses was entrusted to build, according to Exodus 25, was the house of God. The meaning may be even wider. Moses was entrusted with leadership in the whole community of Israel, who had become the people of God's house. The Christian church, as the new Israel, owes much to Moses.

Hebrews contrasts Jesus with Moses. The statement *yet Jesus*, in Greek, balances two phrases that begin with *more*. Jesus has been counted worthy (as has already been stated in 2:9) of *more glory*, as the builder of a house has more honor than the house. The contrast is illustrated by two other phrases in which the key words are *faithful* and *house*. Moses was faithful in all God's house as a servant (verse 5), but *Christ was faithful over God's house as a son* (verse 6). Moses was a servant in God's house, but Christ was the son over it. The word used for *servant* here (see Numbers 12:7) is used in Greek for servants of high rank. Hebrews does not downplay Moses. It honors him. It simply contrasts him with the *son* who is overseer of the house, in charge of all servants in it.

Moses' task as a servant in God's house was to testify to the things that were to be spoken later. Moses' testimony was to what God spoke to him on Mount Sinai, the law God entrusted to him. Many have puzzled over the form of the words *that were to be spoken later*. Does this phrase refer to what would be said in the future, or to things God would say at some future time? The answer becomes clear later in the sermon where the writer explains that the law is just a shadow, an imperfect copy, which becomes clarified by the reality that it copied. What God spoke of old through prophets like Moses foreshadowed the ultimate full word that would later be spoken through Christ (1:2). The law is a forecast of what God will say more perfectly in Christ.

And what is the house in which Moses serves and Christ oversees? We are his house. That is to say, we are God's house if we hold firmly to our Christian faith. Christian faith is based on confident hope, because we are sure of the trustworthiness of God. The word Hebrews uses here for *confidence* had become frequent among Christians in the assurance of their new faith. It meant an assurance in speaking out in public. Hebrews urges it on the Christians for whom the sermon is written and who have become fainthearted. The same emphasis belongs to the word *pride*, which was often used to express exultation. We have a *hope* we cannot keep secret, but about which we are jubilant. We can publicly take *pride in our hope*, or, as the Apostle Paul said, we can *rejoice in our hope of sharing the glory of God* (Romans 5:2). Our present joy is our anticipation of the salvation which will be ours in the heavenly future if we hold fast.

§ § § § § § §

The Message of Hebrews 2

This is the heart of the message in Hebrews: God wants to draw us away from our destructive sin. God's offer of salvation is the most serious and urgent opportunity we will ever have. To miss it, to let our lives drift along without accepting it, is the worst tragedy that could happen to us.

The offer of salvation is to wipe away the sins that destroy us and separate us from God. The offer is clear in what Jesus proclaimed through what he was and what he did in his incarnation. He became one with humanity, suffering the common human experiences, even of temptation. In so doing, in sympathy with our human need for God, through his death he broke the barrier our sins had built up between us and God. We have the record of this from the people who knew Jesus personally. In many ways God has continued to verify what Jesus presented to us, especially by the gifts of the Holy Spirit, who carries on God's purpose among us. We can receive this salvation by trusting Jesus Christ, who is uniquely close to God, because he carried through what God appointed him to do.

Moses was a great religious leader, faithful in God's house. Christ, however, is superior to Moses, faithful to God over his house. We can be thankful for all religious leaders who are faithful to God, but as Christ is superior to all, it is to him we must be faithful. Moses foreshadowed what was to come in God's word. But Christ *is* the perfect word of God to us.

We, Christians, are God's house. We are God's people. We are, that is, if we hold firmly to our faith.

§ § § § § § §

PART THREE Hebrews 3:7–4:13

Introduction to These Chapters

The author explains the promise and warning to be found in the story of Israel's faithlessness in the desert (Exodus 15:23-25; 17:2-7; Psalm 95:8-11). The promise is of a goal, a place of arrival God has prepared for the people, called by Hebrews a *rest*. The entire argument goes like this:

Those to whom the promise was first made lost it through disobedience;
God's true rest is the eternal sabbath rest;
God's word can discern our real intentions.
Here is an outline of Hebrews 3:7–4:13.

    I. Israel Spoiled Its Chance (3:7-11)
   II. Let Us Not Spoil Our Chance (3:12-15)
  III. The People Missed God's Rest (3:16-19)
  IV. God's Rest Is Still Available (4:1-2)
   V. God's Eternal Sabbath Rest (4:3-5)
  VI. The Opportunity Remains (4:6-7)
 VII. God's Rest Is Greater (4:8-10)
VIII. Strive to Enter God's Rest (4:11)
  IX. The Word of God Knows Us (4:12-13)

Israel Spoiled Its Chance (3:7-11)

The writer begins here the second warning and counsel of the sermon (3:7–4:13), comparing Israel's experience in the desert with that of Christians in the world. The danger of not holding fast is illustrated by a passage from the Psalms (Psalm 95:7-11). It is, according to Jewish and

Christian belief at that time, the Holy Spirit that is speaking in the Scriptures (10:15).

The psalm tells of an unhappy event in the wilderness (as recorded in Exodus 15:23-25). The Israelites had been wandering in the desert of Shur for three days without water to drink. The thirsty Israelites reached an oasis called Marah (translated as *bitterness*). The water there was bitter, however, and the people could not drink it. This put them in a bad humor. They were exasperated. They forgot all the wonders God had performed, and they murmured against their leader, Moses (see Numbers 14:26). Psalm 95 gives two other place names, Meribah and Massah, mentioned in Exodus 17. At these places the Israelites complained because there was no water. These names were translated in the Greek Bible, which the author of Hebrews read, as *rebellion* (against God) and as *testing*, words that implied provocation of God and testing God.

According to Psalm 95, the people tested God's patience with them. They *put me to the test*. The psalm quotes Exodus 17:2, where Moses shouts back at the complaining Israelites, *"Why do you put the LORD to the proof?"* The people were losing faith in their goal, as though the proof of it would be the absence of difficulty along the way. The way of faithfulness is not a way of ease. The remainder of Psalm 95 and the real thrust behind Hebrews' treatment of it is based on Numbers 14. The entire dramatic story in Numbers 14 should be read to understand the full force of the warning in Hebrews. The Israelites had arrived near Kadesh on the borders of Canaan, the land God had promised them. Spies brought reports of the fertility and fruitfulness of the land, but also of the strength of its fortifications. Fainthearted, the Israelites were frightened and murmured that they preferred to go back to Egypt, back to slavery. The Lord said, *How long will this people despise me? And how long will they not believe in me, in spite of the signs which I have wrought among them?* (Numbers 14:11). *Your dead bodies shall fall in this wilderness . . . not one shall come into the land where I swore that I would make you dwell . . . .* (Numbers 14:29-30). So they wandered in the desert forty more years, until that generation had died off. As the psalmist quoted by Hebrews put it: *As I swore in my wrath, "They shall never enter my rest."*

The word *rest*, which appears frequently in the Old Testament stories, becomes a key word in Hebrews, Chapter 4. It echoes Deuteronomy 12:9, *to the rest and the inheritance which the* LORD *your God gives you.*

The *rest* God had planned for them was Canaan, *a land which flows with milk and honey* (Numbers 14:8), where the difficulty of a wandering life in the desert would be over. They were not worthy of it, however. They would never enter it. They provoked God for forty years. Hebrews runs the words *for forty years* with the previous line in the psalm: *They saw my works for forty years.* Yet they lost their trust in God and lost their chance.

Let Us Not Spoil Our Chance (3:12-15)

Today, says the psalmist, listen to God and do not harden yourselves, or you also will suffer God's displeasure. God speaks, but the trouble is that the people do not listen. They are heedless.

The preacher of Hebrews is concerned at Christians' faint-heartedness and potential apostasy which may prevent their entering their heavenly home. The danger is the evil, unbelieving heart. It is *unbelief* (verse 19) that prevents entry into God's promised rest. Using words from the psalm, the writer warns Christians, *Do not harden your hearts.* To emphasize the immediacy of the danger of falling away from the living God, the writer twice repeats *today* (verses 13, 15). Tomorrow may be too late; they may have drifted too far (2:1). Every day Christians are to *exhort* (counsel, warn) one another, the author says. Each Christian has a responsibility to encourage other believers. The basis for this encouragement is the supremacy of Christ. Your hearts can so easily grow hardened if you let sin deceive you (verse 13). *Deceitfulness* is an apt word. It describes the way sin can delude and seduce Christians into admitting into their lives the very sins they once would have rejected.

Verse 14 repeats the anxiety expressed in verse 6: *If only we hold our first confidence firm to the end.* This is like Paul's appeal: *O foolish Galatians! Who has bewitched you?* (Galatians 3:1). There must have been a time when their faith was stronger (6:10-11). The call for firmness is frequent in this letter. They can be firm in the faith, *for we share in Christ*. They are comrades together in Christ. The author had said that Christ *partook* of human nature (2:14). Now, using the same verb (although translated *share* in the Revised Standard Version), he says that Christians partake of Christ. This partnership the author shares with those addressed in the sermon, saying *we*, not *you*, and *brethren*, the all-inclusive word for fellow Christians.

The word for *confidence* used here means the personal conviction we had from the beginning in the reality of God reflected in Christ. It is confidence firm to the end because it is confidence in the end. It is the hope (11:1) that supports faithfulness and perseverence.

The People Missed God's Rest (3:16-19)

In three questions with three answers, Hebrews makes three points in the story of the Israelites at Marah. (1) Who *heard* God's voice (verse 7), yet rebelled? Answer: those who had been liberated from Egypt. (2) Who angered God in the wilderness? Answer: those who sinned. (3) Who did not enter God's rest? Answer: those who, because of unbelief, were disobedient.

The three points are applicable to the Christians: (1) They had been saved, liberated from sin; (2) they too, could fall away from God; and (3) that would keep them from the rest God had planned.

In the Old Testament rebellion, idolatry, and sin are often almost synonymous. The story selected by Hebrews of Israel murmuring in the desert illustrates this. God had saved them. God had protected them. God had guided them. Yet, when troubled, they murmured against God. They heard. They had been warned. Yet they were rebellious.

God was *provoked* with those who sinned. He was not against them. Clearly he was for them, and had marvelously delivered them (verses 9-10) in all righteousness. It was because of their sin that God was angry. They *sinned* (verse 17). They were *disobedient* (verse 18). Sin is disobedience, a turning away from God. Their bodies fell in the wilderness because they had fallen *away from the living God* (verse 12). Sin is its own punishment because it comes through *unbelief* (verse 19), which is a failure of faith resulting in faithlessness to God. Verse 19 is a summary of the points of the story and leads to its application in Hebrews 4:1-13.

God's Rest Is Still Available (4:1-2)

This passage corresponds to the previous warning in 2:13. The promise of entering God's rest *remains*. God's promise is still in force. The same word *declared by angels* (2:2) is the good news that came to us. The good news that was brought to them, news of God's promise in Christ, is allegorically linked with the message that the Israelites heard. It is the same promise, given to the Israelites in the desert, that we can enter God's rest. Entering God's rest is our vocation as Christians, our calling from God (3:1). This good news cannot be taken lightly. We are reminded that God's promise to the Israelites was of no use to them. It did not benefit them even though God had intended it for them. That was because, although they heard the good news, they were out of contact with God, who spoke the good news. The hearers had no faith in the speaker of the message. The lines of communication were down. There was no faith for the message to meet or combine with. Another possible interpretation would be that there was a faith basis, such as a system of belief, but what they heard did not combine with that faith. Message and faith did not mix, a typical phenomenon where believers hear but do not assimilate what they hear. Hence, the appropriateness of the admonition in 2:1: We must pay closer attention to what we have heard.

It could happen to you, says the writer of Hebrews. In fact, let us fear lest we not reach our goal. The writer expresses anxiety that some of us might come short of the goal God has set for us, and so not get in. The good news, God's promise (as Hebrews usually puts it), is only for people of faith who believe it and who have confidence in Jesus and conform their lives to that promise. *Let us fear* begins the sentence in the Greek text. *Be judged* translates not as a judgment or a condemnation, but a supposition. Hebrews hints that some Christians (notice the change to second person: *any of you*) might have failed to reach it. The Greek verb here has the connotation of neglect, or drifting, or letting go, already suggested in 2:1-3.

God's Eternal Sabbath Rest (4:3-5)

We enter that rest is the opening phrase in the Greek, used as a contrast to God's statement, *they shall never enter my rest*, from Psalm 95:11. The contrast is between *we who have believed* and those who *failed to enter because of disobedience* (verse 6). Our belief is not simply a past experience, but an ongoing one.

In the reference to the Israelites in the desert, *rest* is the promised land toward which they were journeying. Now the writer definitely associates *rest* with the first sabbath, the seventh day after Creation. *He has somewhere spoken,*

Hebrews says in a typical quotation style. The reference is to Genesis 2:2. God created the universe in a series of six days, says Genesis, *and on the seventh day God finished his work which he had done, and he rested on the seventh day from all his work which he had done.* Many Jewish teachers called this day "the Great Sabbath." *God's works were finished* underlines the origin of the sabbath rest.

The quotation from Psalm 95:11 is followed by the phrase *although his works were finished from the foundation of the* [material] *world.* This asserts that the rest was already waiting for God's people. After all his works, the time of rest had arrived. God rested, and opened up that rest to the people. They shied away from it, drifted off from it, because of lack of faith.

The writer's remarks about Creation are not intended to suggest that God is an absent God who has gone off to take a permanent rest and is unavailable to people. God has a continuing concern for the creation. In the Gospel of John, which has many similarities to Hebrews, Jesus is quoted: *My Father is working still, and I am working* (John 5:17).

The Opportunity Remains (4:6-7)

The point here is that God's rest was already in place long before the time of Moses and the Exodus of Israel from Egypt, in fact, from the seventh day following creation. It was this rest, Hebrews now argues, that the Israelites did not and do not enter (verse 5). It is this sabbath rest that is still available *for some to enter it*.

Hebrews repeats the statement that those for whom the rest was originally intended failed to enter because of disobedience, so God set another day, another opportunity for others to enter it. *Disobedience* is parallel to *unbelief* (3:19) and *hardened hearts* (3:15)—a willful failure to trust God. The Israelites in the desert forgot God's goodness and rebelled against the hardships which were an inevitable part of the liberation towards which God, through Moses, was leading them. Later in the sermon the writer will make more of the essential place suffering has in the Christian experience.

All psalms were accepted by this time as written by David where not explicitly stated otherwise (*Saying through David*, verse 7). Since all the Scriptures are God's word, writers like David were considered to be spokesmen for God, that is, prophets. David, on behalf of God, was urging the people of his time *so long afterward* not to harden their hearts as their ancestors had in the desert.

The word *today* (Psalm 95:7) is repeated twice.

Again he sets a certain day reminds us of Jesus' parable of the banquet invitation: *Come, for all is now ready*. Those invited made excuses, and they refused to come. So in anger the host said, *None of those . . . invited shall taste my banquet*. The invitation was given to others (Luke 14:16-27). Christians felt that the Jewish people had rejected God by rejecting Christ. Through Christ, God had called the Christians to be God's people. In the shadow of this good news lurks the warning: You could miss being God's people, too, if you disobey.

The word *today* emphasizes both the renewed opportunity and the urgency of the good news. The form of the verb *to enter* in Greek suggests immediateness, that the promised opportunity to enter remains but will not be a continuing one. Hebrews is saying that as the people of Israel failed to enter (this rest), so now God *again sets a certain day* for Christians to enter it.

God's Rest Is Greater (4:8-10)

Joshua and *Jesus* are spelled the same in Greek. Hebrews uses the sameness of the name to contrast the first Jesus (Joshua) and the second Jesus, who is Christ. The first led the Israelites, after Moses' death, into the Promised Land. Jesus leads people to the true rest.

The *rest*, which was the Promised Land of Canaan into

which Joshua led his people (the second generation of the desert Israelites), was not the true rest. *If* (verse 8) is the first of several *ifs* in which Hebrews points out the inadequacies of the copy. The inadequacy of the rest in Canaan points to the need of a true rest. *If* it had been the true rest, *God would not speak later of another day*. *Another day* parallels *a certain day* in verse 7. As in 3:5, the writer is speaking of a fulfillment yet to come. The true rest, the sabbath rest, is what is still available for the people of God, the Christians.

This is the third time Hebrews says that a rest *remains*, or still awaits, the people of God. Jewish rabbis argued whether sabbath rest meant the seventh day when God rested from creation or the great Day of the Lord yet to come as the perfect rest. The writer of Hebrews linked the two together. God's sabbath rest *from the foundation of the world* (verse 3) is the rest which the people of God will enter at the end time. It is to this perfect rest that Jesus Christ, in contrast to Joshua, leads his people. The writer probably had read a popular book, Fourth Esdras, in which was this promise of paradise: "Paradise is open to you, and in it is planted the tree of life . . . and its enjoyment is ready, and the city is built, and the rest is appointed for you" (4 Esdras 8:52). The sabbath rest, says Hebrews, is ready for faithful Christians when they have finished their work. Here they will share with God the true peace and bliss of his rest forever.

Strive to Enter God's Rest (4:11)

Hebrews concludes the statement about God's rest by urging Christians to strive to enter it. The word for *strive* means to be eager to enter. Since it is a question of gaining or losing eternal rest, it becomes a matter of priority on the part of Christians to enter that rest. Laxness, indifference to its importance, could mean *to fall by the same sort of disobedience* that excluded the Hebrews in the wilderness.

There is no suggestion in Hebrews that the rest is idleness or the absence of vitality and activity. Psalm 16:9-11 characterizes *God's rest* as Hebrews envisions it:

Therefore my heart is glad, and my soul rejoices;
  my body also dwells secure.
For thou dost not give me up to Sheol,
  or let thy godly one see the Pit.
Thou dost show me the path of life;
  in thy presence there is fulness of joy,
  in thy right hand are pleasures for evermore.

The Word of God Knows Us (4:12-13)

A final word of warning is given to Christians against the danger of falling into *disobedience.*

Christianity is nothing to trifle with. God is not fooled by superficial religion. This passage is like Paul's warning: *Be not deceived; God is not mocked* (Galatians 6:7). It is like Psalm 139 with which the author of Hebrews was undoubtedly familiar: *Thou knowest when I sit down and when I rise up; thou discernest my thoughts from afar.*

The *word of God* is not a dead, passive word. It is alive and effective. It is living and active. It enters the very depths of our being. The word of God is compared to a *two-edged sword.* This was a common metaphor. The author knew Isaiah 49:2: *He made my mouth like a sharp sword.* A sharp, two-edged sword comes out of the mouth of the figure in the vision of John of Patmos (Revelation 1:16). Just as a sharp sword, piercing the body, separates and exposes the flesh in its very deepest hidden parts, *the joints and marrow,* so God's word exposes our inner thoughts and intentions, our desires and will, to God's scrutiny. The soul and spirit suggest the flowing energy of life, which is pierced when the body is pierced. The heart, in the time of Hebrews, signified the mental, the intellectual, and the emotional activity of a person. In the heart are found the attitudes and motives of a person. They may be hidden from other people, but not from

God. In fact, *no creature*, nothing in all creation, is hidden. On the contrary, *all are open* (the word for *naked* is used here) and *laid bare to the eyes of God*. Because *laid bare* is a term used in wrestling matches, some students of Hebrews have suggested that the writer had in mind the picture of God throwing down those who stand against the divine will, overthrowing them and laying them bare.

Of him with whom we have to do can be translated *of him to whom we must give account*.

§ § § § § § §

The Message of Hebrews 3:7–4:13

We need to remember what happened to the Israelites when they traveled to the Promised Land of Canaan. Miraculously God had liberated them from slavery, guided them, protected them, and provided for them.

§ Nevertheless, when facing difficulties—lack of drinkable water in a desert oasis, the dangers of entering a new land—they did not stop to consider all that God had done and could do for them. They complained, rebelled, were disobedient, and sinned against God.

§ Then God knew they were unworthy to enter the rest that was planned for them. They died in the desert.

The same thing, figuratively, could happen to us.

§ Through Christ we have been freed from sin, and drawn together and to God.

§ If, however, we become careless about our faith, losing the confidence we had when we first believed, we can be deceived by sin and we can drift away from God.

§ Then, like the Israelites in the desert, we may never experience the eternal rest God has planned for us.

In Genesis we read that God rested on the seventh day after having created the world. This sabbath rest of God is from the beginning and lasts forever. It is part of God's plan. God not only created the universe, but also set up a goal for the creation. That goal is reached in the ultimate, eternal communion with God's chosen people. Work was not to be an end in itself, but a creative movement toward the rest shared by God with the people. Those first chosen failed to reach it because of disobedience. Nevertheless, God has opened up the possibility of this rest to all who will be faithful. That rest, God's rest, remains for us to enter.

§ § § § § § §

PART FOUR Hebrews 4:14–5:10

Introduction to These Chapters

The admonition in 3:7–4:13 concluded with an urging to enter God's rest. That entry, drawing near to God, is made possible by Jesus' high priestly act. This passage explains how Jesus became our great high priest. The high priest in Israel's sanctuary served as mediator for the people's sins as well as for his own sins before God. High priests were appointed for their task. Jesus was appointed by God, and became the perfect high priest to mediate our sins. He became high priest by humbling himself and suffering in obedience to God. He became like us, except that he did not sin. Hebrews explains this to encourage faithfulness and obedience to Christ as a sure way to draw near to God to receive God's grace and mercy.

Here is an outline of Hebrews 4:14–5:10.
 I. In Faith Draw Near to God (4:14-16)
 II. High Priests Are Appointed (5:1-4)
 III. God Appointed Christ High Priest (5:5-6)
 IV. Jesus Is Our Perfect High Priest (5:7-10)

In Faith Draw Near to God (4:14-16)

These three verses are the kernel of the message of Hebrews, and an introduction to the third lesson: how Jesus became our high priest. Jesus is the basis for confidence in holding true to our faith. Jesus understands our human experience because he was human (see 2:17) without sinning. He understands our struggle with sin, because he has been tempted. He did not give in to temptation. He is the high priest of our confession, the faith to which we have committed ourselves (3:1). From here through Chapter 10, the meaning of Jesus, a high priest of our confession, is explained. His complete obedience to God involved him in suffering (2:9-10, 14-18). And so he *has passed through the heavens,* penetrating to the very presence of God. The imagery is that of the high priest penetrating the curtain in the sanctuary into the Most Holy Place to come into the presence of God. (Hebrews explains and expands this image later in the sermon, in 9:1-14.) That is why Jesus is the *great high priest.* No earthly high priest has been able to approach so close to God in behalf of us sinners. Only Christ has arrived there (6:19-20; 9:24) for the perfect priestly act.

Hebrews has written about a *Son* (1:2, 5, 8) through whom God speaks to us, about Jesus who suffered and died, faithful to God (2:9-10), and was also called Christ (God's anointed Messiah, 3:6, 14). Now Hebrews clearly identifies Jesus as the *Son of God.*

Some people were saying that if Jesus was divine, he could not have understood our human predicament. He was fully human, says the writer of Hebrews. Of no angel, and of none of the many savior gods of religion in the Mediterranean world or anywhere else could this be said: that in full humanity he knew human weaknesses and temptation. Like us, he knew human frailties. Jesus can, therefore, sympathize, and feel with us our pain, weakness, and need (see Matthew 8:17). Jesus walked where we walk, experienced our experiences, was limited by our limitations, suffered as we suffer. He understands. (See 2:18.)

Bodily weaknesses indicate human limitations of all kinds. It is these weaknesses that make human beings vulnerable to temptation. One does not have to give in to know the threat and danger of sin. It is such experiences that put us to the proof. Jesus did not surrender to them, thus proving his worthiness to be high priest to the rest of us who do.

Without sin could be translated *apart from sin*. Whoever does an act of sin, in that action draws away from God. Jesus could have sinned. That possibility is essential to what Hebrews is saying. He kept apart from sin because he kept in touch with God. The temptations of concern to Hebrews are those that can draw Christians away from faithfulness to Christ to *falling away* and to *disobedience*.

With such a one to represent us, who was from God yet became as we are, we can hold fast our confession, that to which we have committed ourselves. *Let us then with confidence draw near to the throne of grace*. This line, more than any, sums up the theme of Hebrews. This word *confidence*, a favorite with Hebrews, includes the boldness of open public confession, as well as the assurance of trust and communion with God.

In verse 16 we can picture a supplicant coming humbly before the highest authority where he is sure he will be received despite his bad record. God's awesome glory upon the throne (depicted in Psalm 29) and God's righteousness make it unthinkable that smallness and unrighteousness could come near God.

Nevertheless, despite your sins and weaknesses, you can, says Hebrews to the hesitant Christians, draw near to God confidently. The verb indicates a continual drawing near to God. Faith is a daily exercise of growing trust. Your confidence is not in yourself. That would be arrogance. Your confidence is in God's grace. The Old Testament refers several times to a *throne of honor* (Isaiah 22:23) as a mark of royal splendor and greatness. Hebrews modifies the phrase to *the throne of grace*. Here God sits and responds with mercy to those who come near. Because of what Christ has done for them, as their perfect high priest, they will receive mercy, compassion, forgiveness of sin, and *find grace to help in time of need*, in time of trial and temptation. The greater the need, the greater the grace. This echoes the author's Greek text of Proverbs 8:17: *And those who seek me will find* [grace]. The God of the Old Testament is a God who cares about and helps the poor and oppressed. The God of Hebrews cares enough, even for sinners, to send the Son to make a way for them to be free of their sin and enter the presence of God's righteousness.

High Priests Are Appointed (5:1-4)

What is a high priest? The sermon outlines the character and work of the high priest according to the Old Testament. First, he is a human being chosen from among human beings to represent them in whatever pertains to their relationship with God.

Second, he makes sacrifices as a way of expressing the people's repentance and appeal for forgiveness. Since they are always breaking their relationship with God, they must bring gifts and sacrifices for sins. These were animals specified by the worship code, brought as a penance for involuntary sins, for temporary slips, but not for obstinate intention to violate God's will. Hardness of heart and disobedience, the sins which kept the Israelites out of God's rest (3:18-19), were not included. The high priest sprinkled the blood of the sacrificed animal in the Most Holy Place of the sanctuary, and the people's sins were absolved.

Third, he had to be someone who would have sympathetic understanding of human weakness. *He can deal gently* could be translated literally, *He can feel in due measure* (with neither cold indifference nor indulgent permissiveness) the ignorance and waywardness of the people. After all, the high priest himself is beset with weakness pressing in from every side. The *ignorant* who sin *unwittingly* (Leviticus 4:1) lack an understanding of the law. The *wayward* are led astray by the *deceitfulness of sin* (3:13).

Fourth, he is bound to offer sacrifices for his own sins as well, otherwise his sacrifices on behalf of other people would not be acceptable (Leviticus 4:1-3).

Fifth, the high priest is not his own person. He *does not take the honor upon himself*—this great responsibility. He does not do it for personal ambition. He is *appointed* (verse 1), *called by God*, and must fit the divine requirements. According to Leviticus 8, Aaron, brother of Moses, was designated high priest of the Hebrews. The office was passed down to Aaron's heirs.

In this description, Hebrews stresses the limitations of the high priest: human, a sinner, chosen, appointed, and temporary.

God Appointed Christ High Priest (5:5-6)

So also, Christ fit the pattern of the priesthood. How like, yet how different, was his priesthood! He also did not choose to be high priest for his self-exaltation. Hebrews uses the Greek verb *to glorify*. Jesus did not seek the glory associated with this high office. *He was appointed by him who said to him . . . .* The author cites the words of Psalm 2:7, where God declares the messiah to be *my Son*.

The early Christians repeatedly insisted that their religion was not one of human design, but God's. Thus, Hebrews says Christ was no self-made priest or self-proclaimed prophet. He was appointed by God. *For we did not follow cleverly devised myths when we made known to you the power and coming of our Lord Jesus Christ* (2 Peter 1:16).

Psalm 110:4 is quoted in verse 6. This passage is important because the author will add several paragraphs explaining how it applies to Christ. God appoints Christ to be a high priest not of the descendants of Aaron, but like Melchizedek. The 110th psalm is a late psalm. The story of Melchizedek was an ancient one, written into the story of Abraham (Genesis 14:18-20). Melchizedek was both king and priest. Many early kings in the Middle East were the high priests of their people. The significance was that someone outside the family of Abraham—and not just his descendants—could be priests of the Most High God and receive honor and tithes from Abraham. Psalm 110 celebrated the ideal king in Jerusalem who would combine in himself, like Melchizedek (thought to be a pre-Israelite king of Jerusalem), the functions of king and high priest. Because Psalm 110:4 was considered to be about the messiah, the writer of Hebrews finds the reference to Melchizedek a good one for developing his ideas of Christ as a priest-king different from the old priesthood of Israel.

Jesus Is Our Perfect High Priest (5:7-10)

Jesus fit the pattern of high priesthood by his ability to sympathize with human need and suffering. *In the days of his flesh*, that is, during his incarnation on earth, focuses on the story, apparently well-known by then, of Jesus' agony in the garden of Gethsamane. In the intensity of this experience, Christ knew what it was to suffer *with loud cries and tears*. Through it all his attention was fixed on God, on *him who was able to save him from death*, and he *was heard for his godly fear*. The writer knew Jesus was not saved from death. The cross is not mentioned, yet the crucifixion is understood as the climax of Jesus' obedient human suffering. The Greek word here for *fear* was often used to mean human anxiety about pain, shame, and death. It was from this fear that God saved Jesus, as the Gospel stories show.

Hebrews understands the significance of this prayer. Even those with strong faith would like to avoid pain, and everyone has some fear of death. Jesus' reaction is typically human. Crucifixion is an exceeding agony, as well as a public spectacle of ignominy. But Jesus trusted God. Jesus' prayers and supplications were not that God do Jesus' will. Rather, it was that Jesus might, whatever the outcome, do God's will (see Mark 14:36).

Although he was a Son (verse 8), *he learned obedience through what he suffered.* Among the contemporaries of the first-century Christians were devotees—as there were and still are in Asia—of redeemer gods and goddesses who never became truly and completely human, so that any suffering in their stories was no more than stage play. As a human person, Jesus had the learning experience that comes with suffering and obedience. Suffering can lead a person to negative ends such as anger and bitterness. But Jesus learned obedience through suffering. The word *obedience* could be translated into the old English word *heeding*. Jesus heeded, listened to God through all his suffering. That is how, Hebrews says, Jesus came to be appointed by God a high priest like Melchizedek. *To all who obey him* (the tense is present, implying continual obedience), who continue to heed, to listen, to keep their attention fixed on him, Jesus *became the source of eternal salvation.* Salvation is the rest Hebrews has been talking about. It is eternal well-being, living with God forever.

§ § § § § § §

The Message of Hebrews 4:14–5:10

We can have confidence that Christ, as a high priest for us in God's presence, helps us in our spiritual lives because:

§ He was appointed by God to relate us to God;

§ He was obedient to God, although this meant that he suffered agony in his human incarnation;

§ He shared the weakness of human limitations;

§ He was tempted, but he passed through this incarnation experience perfectly, and was raised into God's presence;

§ He is a perfect high priest, who intercedes for us, because

§ He understands our human problems, so

§ He can relate us to God, and

§ He will always be our source for eternal salvation. However, we, who are weak, tempted, and lack knowledge, must:

§ Hold fast to the faith we have;

§ Let it dominate our lives as we keep on drawing closer to God every day;

§ Expose our needs to God;

§ Accept God's forgiving grace and mercy for daily living;

§ Let Christ be the source of our ongoing faith;

§ Daily obey what we learn through Jesus Christ.

§ § § § § § §

PART FIVE Hebrews 5:11–6:8

Introduction to These Chapters

The writer of Hebrews pauses abruptly, like a speaker who has lost the listeners' attention, and stops to chide them for their dullness. They may be too immature to understand the message. What is worse, they are immature in their Christianity.

This is the third, and sternest, warning of the sermon. It begins with a scolding. They have been Christians long enough. But there they are, still going over their ABC's of faith, hardly knowing the difference between right and wrong. They dabble in foolish speculations.

Mature persons cannot become immature. They cannot lose their faith and begin over again. People produce what is inside of them, good or bad. In 5:9 the writer has said that Jesus became *the source of eternal salvation to all who obey him*. There are doubts, however, about the Christians making use of this source, and hence about their maturing toward eternal salvation.

Here is an outline of Hebrews 5:11–6:8.
I. You Should Be Mature (5:11-14)
II. Let Us Go On to Maturity (6:1-3)
III. You Cannot Begin Again (6:4-6)
IV. Land Produces Good Crops or Weeds (6:7-8)

You Should Be Mature (5:11-14)

You have been Christians for a long time, says Hebrews. By this time you should be able to understand all that I have to say to you about this. In fact, you should now be able to teach God's word—the Scriptures that the writer is explaining. *It is hard to explain.* Second Peter 3:15-16 says this of Paul's simpler writing. The author's reasoning was typical of the rabbis of his day. Did he fear it was too complicated? If the author was Apollos, as some think, whose brilliant preaching dazzled some Corinthian Christians (1 Corinthians 1:12, 17; 2:1), he may have wondered if he was too intellectual for the simple audience he was addressing. Paul seems to have discounted the wisdom of Apollos in comparison with the simple gospel Paul was preaching (1 Corinthians 1:17–2:5). The real reason, says the writer of Hebrews, is that they have become *dull of hearing.* In lifestyles that slip into the neglect of faith and hope, spiritual and moral awareness grows dull and sluggish. The writer detects and deplores this dullness of undertanding among the readers. They must have been like the Galatian Christians whom Paul scolded for being so easily drawn away from their faith (Galatians 5:4, 5).

You ought to be teachers was a phrase of rebuke to persons who were slow in speaking out confidently what they had learned. You are like babies; you need someone to teach you again the first principles, the ABC's of your religion. These were Christians who knew no more about their faith many years later than when they first became Christians. We have the imagery here of an adult who tries to live on milk. *You need milk, not solid food.* Like infants who cannot discern good from bad, they are *unskilled in the word of righteousness.* (Note Paul's similar remarks to Corinthian Christians who were like babies on milk, not ready for solid food, 1 Corinthians 3:1-2.)

The mature, by contrast, are those who have their faculties trained by practice. They have exercised their moral muscles to distinguish good from evil. The *word of righteousness* may also mean, for the author, religious teaching about Christ's high priesthood which leads to a life of faith (11:7; 12:11).

Let Us Go On to Maturity (6:1-3)

However immature the people are, the writer is not going to give them more milk, or go over the first principles. Solid food is in order. The Greek for *let us go on* is, literally, *let us be carried* or *let us carry ourselves*. In Ephesians 4:14-15 we read: . . . *that we may no longer be children, tossed to and fro and carried about by every wind of doctrine . . . Rather . . . we are to grow up*. This sermon is saying: Let us grow up.

The elementary doctrines of Christ were foundation stones. Foundations are necessary but the structure is never built if we do not get beyond laying and relaying the foundation. What were those foundations? Hebrews mentions them briefly in order to hurry on to more important teaching. There are six elements listed in a rhythm of pairs.

(1) . . . *of repentance from dead works*. In Ephesians 2:1, repentance is characterized as being *made alive, when you were dead through the trespasses and sins in which you once walked*. Dead works were the actions of those not alive in Christ. Therefore, as far as Christians were concerned, they were *the fleeting pleasures of sin* (11:25). New Christians were no doubt taught clearly that to be Christians, certain activities, occupations, and interests which belonged to worldly culture about them had to be abandoned. They contaminated a person, as a dead body was supposed to contaminate the living. The problems church leaders had with the church in Corinth (raised in 1 and 2 Corinthians) show that pagans without the background of Jewish moral instruction had difficulty understanding that many practices accepted in their society were unacceptable in the Christian life.

(2) . . . *of faith toward God*. The writer may have written this as faith *toward* rather than simply faith *in* God because, for Hebrews, faith always involves movement toward access to God. That is the direction of the Christian life.

(3) . . . *with instruction about ablutions* (washings, cleansings, baptisms). This follows naturally from the instructions about dead works. Washing is the transition from dead works to faith toward God. Jewish ceremonial law required washing after contact with anything dead (Numbers 19:11-13). Proselytes to Judaism had to be washed, or baptized, before being acceptable. Hebrews will use the idea that Christ will *purify your conscience from dead works to serve the living God* (9:14). Paul writes in the same vein to the Colossians (Colossians 2:12) as does the writer of Hebrews in 10:22. Baptisms (plural) is what the writer is talking about. Just as new Christians had to have it made clear which practices were dead works, they had to be clear about distinguishing Christian baptism from the many religious ceremonial washings of their time. The Pharisees practiced washing ceremonies. The Essenes, a strict Jewish sect, had many ritual washings. Pagan religions had rites in which new members were washed. The difference and significance of Christian baptism had to be explained.

(4) . . . *the laying on of hands*. When the new Christians in Ephesus were baptized again in the name of the Lord Jesus, Paul *laid his hands upon them* and *the Holy Spirit came on them* (Acts 19:6). Paul had been set apart with Barnabas for missionary work at the church in Antioch through the laying on of hands (Acts 13:3). Laying on of hands was practiced from the beginning of Christianity to communicate the Holy Spirit (Acts 8:17-19) and as a consecration for special ministry (1 Timothy 4:14; 5:22; 2 Timothy 1:6). It was a Jewish practice followed by Christians, a special blessing from church leaders.

(5) . . . *the resurrection of the dead*. Most Jews, especially Pharisees, believed in the resurrection of the dead. The concept was different from a popular concept of immortality in many cults. For Christians, resurrection of the body was associated with the resurrection of Christ and with his impending return. The need of new

Christians to understand this idea is seen in Paul's explanations to the Thessalonians and the Corinthians (1 Corinthians 15:12-23; 1 Thessalonians 4:13-18).

(6) . . . *eternal judgment* was believed in by both Jews and Christians. For Christians, judgment is related to the return of Christ when the final separation (an old Greek word for *judgment*) will be made between the righteous in Christ and the unrighteous (John 5:28-29). This is the dividing point between the present age and the age to come, as Paul explains to his earthly judge (see Acts 24:15, 25).

The Christians addressed knew what these basic instructions were and Hebrews mentions them only parenthetically. Verse 3, *And this we will do,* continues the urging in verse 1 to *go on to maturity.* We will go to a more mature understanding and practice of faith. What is of concern to the writer is not getting the rudiments of religion right again and again as much as living a life that moves steadily on in faithfulness to Christ. The writer's intention to carry the readers to advanced teaching is made subject to God's will, *if God permits* (James 4:15).

You Cannot Begin Again (6:4-6)

This going on to maturity is the serious matter the author wishes to discuss. There is a conditional threat in these two verses. If you don't move forward, you move backward, and you cannot get started again. It would be impossible. The author of Hebrews was deeply alarmed that the people to whom he was writing might be in danger of abandoning their faith through neglect of it. That is the reason for the sermon (see the Introduction, page 8).

It is impossible begins the sentence. It echoes the frequently repeated phrase in Chapter 3: *They shall never enter my rest. It is impossible,* if they fall away, to be renewed through repentance. Outside of Hebrews, there is no New Testament sentence that carries such potential terror: the warning that salvation could be eternally lost, even to Christians. Several words and phrases in these verses are important clues to what the writer is saying. The long sentence has two parts. The first part (verses 4-5) describes the experience of believing Christians. They *have once been enlightened*. This is Hebrews' word for conversion. Their eyes have been opened to the light of Christ (see 1 John 1:7). This is attested to by baptism, which 1 Peter 2:9 characterizes as being called *out of darkness into his marvelous light*.

They *have tasted the heavenly gift*: *Tasted* means *experienced*. Christians have experienced the gift of salvation, the new life given by God in Christ as a foretaste of heavenly fellowship.

They *have become partakers of the Holy Spirit*: Christian fellowship is a sharing of the Holy Spirit who binds Christians together.

They *have tasted the goodness of the word of God,* experienced the beauty of the gospel in which God has spoken to us through Jesus Christ (1:2). The writer does not use his usual designation for *word* here, but rather a word that implies God's teachings. They have to do with *the age to come. Powers* may refer in general to wonders of the coming age. *Powers*, however, was frequently used as a general term for either divine or demonic forces (Romans 8:38; Ephesians 3:10). In this case, it is the awesome power that is evident in the vicinity of God's felt presence. The messianic age will be fulfilled on Jesus' return. In the meantime, Christians have seen evidence in *signs and wonders* (2:4).

The second part of the sentence tells why they who have once had these experiences, *if they then commit apostasy* (that is, fall away, reject what they once believed), they cannot be restored. This is about defectors from heaven. They have not arrived, but they are in the company of those who are going toward heaven, lit by its radiance, sharing its joy. Then they deliberately turn their backs and walk away from the light into shadows. They cannot be restored. This happens because *they crucify the Son of God on their own account* to their own hurt. What they are doing by rejecting Christ who died for them is approving his crucifixion. Even if non-believers could crucify Christ in their ignorance and could be forgiven (Luke 13:34), these defectors know full well that it is the *Son of God* they are crucifying.

They *hold him up to contempt*: They mock Christ who suffered pain and shame in their behalf. Their public shaming of him is the worst of all because, having been of his company, their repudiation of Christ tells the world that they consider him of no worth. This horrifies the writer.

To restore again to repentance has the greater force in the Greek original in that it comes toward the end of a long sentence. Hebrews' conviction of the decisiveness of denial of Christ reflects the words of Jesus in Matthew 10:33: *Whoever denies me before men, I also will deny before my Father who is in heaven.* The writer does not say here that these persons repent and will not be forgiven. Rather, he says that it is impossible to renew them to repentance, as though heaven would wish to do so, but Christ is dead to them (see 12:16). They have cast him out of their lives. Their hearts are hardened (3:7-9). They have made the ultimate decision. They have, as it were, thrown themselves away. They have lost the ability to repent.

Land Produces Good Crops or Weeds (6:7-8)

The impossibility expressed in verse 4 is here explained. To illustrate, Hebrews tells a parable of a field. With good rainfall, it produces good crops. God says that it is good land. This is like all the good that Christians have experienced from God (6:4-5). Afterward the field begins to produce only *thorns and thistles*. It is no longer acceptable. It is cursed. It is burned over. This image recalls God's cursing the ground of Eden so that it bore only thorns and thistles (Genesis 3:18). Adam and Eve had been the beneficiaries of God's goodness to them, yet they sinned against him.

The parable is a picture of land which has eagerly *drunk the rain* and produced vegetation that is useful, like new, eager Christians. If the same field changes, bearing only thorns and thistles, it is simply no good. That is clearly Hebrews' message to Christians. It is a factual statement. The apostate Christians no longer produce good. They are fit only for the fire. The Bible frequently speaks of the wicked as being cast into the fire. This is an apt illustration, because refuse was burned outside the city. The parable is like Isaiah's parable of the vineyard (Isaiah 5:1-7).

§ § § § § § §

The Message of Hebrews 5:11–6:8

This passage expresses the writer's concern about the immaturity of the Hebrews' faith. They have been Christians a long time, but have never gone beyond the basics of Christianity. By now they should know enough so that they could teach others, yet they appear not even to understand what the author is trying to say about Christ. Hebrews urges them to go on to maturity, warning them that they run the risk of losing salvation altogether if they continue as they are in a downslide which could bring them in the end to betraying Christ.

The author addresses a general problem among Christians. The passage reminds us that:

§ The Christian faith is a sharing of the word of God and of the Holy Spirit of God.

§ The Christian's life is an experience of the goodness of God illuminated by the heavenly eternal life to come with God.

§ Actually, however, many Christians remain immature in faith, spiritually infantile, biblically illiterate, not really understanding the full Christian message.

§ It does not make sense for people simply to go over and over again the ABC's of Christianity, which they understand only in terms of their secular background.

§ Not to move ahead or grow in Christian faith is to become more apt to fall away from it to the point of neglecting or even rejecting it. This kind of life could even bring one to live in contradiction to Christ and the cross.

§ A deliberate rejection of Christ is turning one's back on the saving, liberating possibilities of access to and eternal fellowship with God.

§ § § § § § §

PART SIX Hebrews 6:9-20

Introduction to These Verses

These verses close Hebrews' third section of warning and encouragement (6:9-20).

From warning Christians, the sermon abruptly turns to commending and encouraging the Christians. They are not apostate and beyond hope. They must move more assuredly toward the hope that is set before them. They must imitate people of great faith who have lived before them.

Hebrews, in this section, assures Christians that they can rely on the unchangeable promise of God to bless them. But Christians need faith and patience as Abraham had so that they can follow when Jesus leads them to the presence of God.

Here is the outline for Hebrews 6:9-20.
I. You Have Done Well (6:9-10)
II. Imitate People of Faith (6:11-12)
III. God's Promise to Abraham Was Sure (6:13-15)
IV. God's Purpose Is Doubly Sure (6:16-18)
V. We Can Be Confident (6:18-20)

You Have Done Well (6:9-10)

The writer understands human psychology. We need a strong warning against a danger toward which we may be drifting. All the same, we need encouragement. The good we do should not be overlooked but commended. God is not so unjust as to overlook it.

Although I am talking this way (*Though we speak thus,*

verse 9), I do not mean to frighten you, says the writer. What I am warning you about could happen to Christians, but in your case I expect better things. In calling them *beloved* (dear ones), the word used by Christians in their close fellowship, the writer shows a loving concern for those addressed. He wishes to assure them of his caring and his hope for them. These Christians belong in the good field of the parable told in verses 7-8. They are not producing thorns and thistles. They are, by their loving service to the saints, yielding useful "vegetation," and this gives the writer hope for them. They have shown love, which is the saving grace among Christians.

These *better things* (better than the dire actions listed in verse 6) put them on the side of *salvation*. *Better* (sometimes translated *superior*) appears thirteen times in the sermon. It expresses the Hebrews theme of upward and forward movement. We are living in the days that will consummate the *better*, our salvation (11:40). Now that Christ has come, better than angels (1:4), more glorious than Moses (3:3), better than the priestly descendants of Aaron (7:7), Christ brings us a better hope (7:19), a better covenant (7:26; 8:6) based on a better promise (8:6), effected by a better sacrifice (9:23). We, therefore, like the faithful ones who came before us, go on to a better country (11:16), to greater possessions than the paltry ones of earth (10:34), for we shall rise to a better life (11:35).

Hebrews is about *salvation*. This word appears seven times, although many other words are used for it in translation. *Salvation* means *to be saved*, as Noah and his family were saved at the time of the Flood (11:7). The Hebrews emphasis is on being saved from a corrupt world and for a better one, from the lesser things of this world to the better things. Salvation is the *heavenly gift* mentioned in verse 4. The angels are sent to help us if we are eager to receive salvation (1:14). Christ has made salvation possible for us through his suffering (2:10). Christ, made perfect, is our source of getting salvation, if we obey him (5:9). Christ will appear again to bring salvation to us if we are living expectantly for him (9:28). So great is this offer of salvation, the neglect of it is terrible to contemplate (2:3).

The *saints* are fellow believers. All Christians in congregations (but not as separate individuals) were called *saints* (literally, *holy ones*), consecrated to God and sharing together the Holy Spirit (verse 4). *The saints* was often used in a special sense to designate the first and oldest community of Christians in Jerusalem. In later generations, the term was often used for older pioneers of the faith in the local community, people whose faith deserved imitation.

The *work of love* these Christians did was done *for his sake*, motivated by love for God.

Imitate People of Faith (6:11-12)

It is not enough to do good if you are not also steadily moving upward in faith and hope. The writer expresses a deep desire that *each one of you* carry on and go forward *to show the same earnestness*. The verb *show* parallels *showed* in verse 10. You showed love in serving the saints; show the same eagerness (ardor and sustained effort) in your life of faith to the very end, so that you may realize the full assurance of what you hope for—God's *heavenly gift* (verse 4). Movement toward hope's fulfillment is thematic in the Hebrews sermon. God sets this hope before us in the promises to us (see verse 17). *In realizing the full assurance of hope* is like the prayer in the Ephesians letter, *that you may know what is the hope to which he has called you* (Ephesians 1:18).

In fact, you must move ahead, *so that you may not be* (become) *sluggish*. The same Greek word is translated *dull* in 5:11. Such sluggishness does not occur if you live eagerly in hope. A live hope keeps the spiritual circulation moving. Christians who lose hope, lose out. As a stimulant to keep on moving ahead in the faith, the writer recommends the imitation of those (some of whose stories will be reviewed later, in Chapter 11) *who through faith and patience inherit the promises.*

Inherit and *promise* are important words in Hebrews. *Heir, inherit,* and *inheritance* appear nine times (in Greek), and *promise,* verb and noun, appears nineteen times. The promise of God to Abraham (6:13) was that his descendants would increase greatly and dwell in Canaan (the land of the inherited promise, 11:8-9). This is a symbol of the greater promise to God's people of *entering his rest* (4:1 and Psalm 95:11), described as a *promised eternal inheritance* (9:15).

This *promised inheritance* is the promise that is inherited (6:12, 15). The inheritance (translated in the Revised Standard Version as *obtain*) is defined as *salvation* (1:14), a *blessing* (12:17), and *righteousness* (11:7). This promise is inherited through patience (6:15), endurance (10:36), and through faith (11:33) or, as here, *through faith and patience.*

The word *faith* indicates faith in and faithfulness to Christ. The word *patience,* originally and more literally translated as *longsuffering,* means to remain steadfast no matter what people or events may do to you. It cannot be doubted, as the writer goes on to explain (verses 13-20), that the promise waits ahead for those who move toward it with steadfast faith.

God's Promise to Abraham Was Sure (6:13-15)

One example of a faith-leader to be imitated is Abraham, ancestor of Israel. The emphasis in these verses is on the certainty of God's promise on the one hand, and Abraham's faithful endurance by which he was able to appropriate that promise on the other hand. This reference is to God's promise made to Abraham after Abraham, faithful to God's command, prepared to sacrifice his son, Isaac (Genesis 22:15-18). The promise is:

Surely I will bless you and multiply you. This sworn promise of God which the writer quotes is, in literal translation from his Greek Bible: "In blessing I will bless you; multiplying, I will multiply you." This phrase conveys the immensity of the promise by one who *is able to do far more abundantly than all that we ask or think* (Ephesians 3:20).

A *blessing* is the good things a well-wisher may say. The greater the well-wisher, the greater the power to assure that the good things will occur. When the well-wisher is God (*I will bless you,* verse 14), there is no doubt as to God's power to make the good that he speaks come true. The greatest good that could be wished for in the ancient Middle East would include the assurance of many offspring (*and multiply you,* verse 14).

How did it happen that Abraham *obtained the promise*? He was faithful, he *patiently endured.* The word used here is *longsuffering.* It does not mean "grin and bear it." It means "persevere" in an unfaltering drive that neither lashes out at nor gives in to anyone who tries to put obstacles in the way. Abraham kept the faith. He pressed on. Faithful through all to God, he was confident in God's promise, and obtained it.

God's Purpose Is Doubly Sure (6:16-18)

The writer has already asserted that *it is impossible* (verse 4) to win if you turn away from what God has offered. He now repeats the phrase in a new setting: *It is impossible* (verse 18) to lose if you keep your faith in what God has promised. Hebrews might have added here, as Paul did when writing about God's promise to Abraham, that the words of promise *were written not for his sake alone, but for ours also* (Romans 4:23-24).

These verses accent the irrevocability of God's promise. God has sworn it with an oath. Despite early Christian opposition to oath-taking (Matthew 5:33-37; James 5:12), Hebrews takes the verse in Genesis at its face value (Genesis 22:16). It says: *By myself I have sworn.* God did not swear *by heaven*, or *by earth*, or *by Jerusalem*. There was nothing greater to swear by so God swore *by himself*. An oath is an act of final confirmation. It guarantees what is sworn. That is the important point here. There could be no greater guarantee in the universe than the oath of God. Therefore, nothing could be more sure than what God promises.

The writer switches to *we* and *us*. We can be doubly sure. As God is unchangeable, so God's promise is unchangeable. God does not lie. God's purpose, resolve, and decision are irrevocable. We can depend on these things through two unchangeable elements, God's promise and God's confirming oath.

We Can Be Confident (6:18-20)

God's promise and oath give us powerful encouragement to seize the hope set before us. Who has this promise and oath? *We who have fled for refuge*. This phrase has been variously translated. It carries the image of refugees who have left home, left everything, and are strangers in the land, moving on toward a better country.

The verb for *fleeing* is used only one other place in the New Testament. Paul and Barnabas fled from Iconium. People there were about to stone them and the missionaries *fled* for their lives (Acts 14:6). The emphasis is on *flight from*. Christians must fly from the world. Flight from the world for the Christian is flight to the city of God. In the Acts account, Paul and Barnabas fled from Iconium to the nearby cities of Lystra and Derbe, *and there they preached the gospel* (Acts 14:7). The Christian life is not simply arriving at the goal of the hope set before us, but it involves going there, and living that hope along the way.

Hope, another key word in Hebrews, is not just an attitude of wishful thinking. Hope includes the object of hope. Christians, Hebrews says, live expectantly. The object of hope is reachable, within grasping distance. All we need to do is reach in order to grasp, *seize* that hope. The picture is of a runner stretching every muscle, racing straight toward the goal for the reward which is there. Jesus is called the *forerunner*. He blazes the trail, goes ahead to open up the way. That is our assurance, says the writer of Hebrews, that the goal of our hope is there. In the figure of the high priest, Hebrews dramatizes what is expressed in John 14:2: *I go to prepare a place for you* (in my Father's house).

The metaphor in verse 19 may be mixed, but the idea is clear. The anchor that penetrates beyond the curtain of the sanctuary is our hope. An anchor firmly imbedded in the sands keeps the ship from drifting and can be used to draw the boat to its mooring even when the mists hide it. The assurance we have in God's promise gives us a firmly fixed anchorage of hope. So we do not drift. The figure of the *anchor of the soul* was frequent in contemporary Greek literature, and was often an image set up beside Christian graves. The writer to the Hebrews is assuring us, Christians, that whatever the storms of life, the *soul*, the human spirit, is safe and secure through hope.

We already live by hope. We do not see the goal toward which we move, but we will actually arrive there when we are perfected forever through Christ. Jesus, like a high priest, has already entered into the inner shrine behind the curtain. This illustration is taken from the plan of the sanctuary of Israel. In the curtained-off room, called the Most Holy Place, the high priest entered into God's presence. (See the comments on Hebrews 5:3.) There, in the true heavenly sanctuary, Jesus intercedes for us that we, following him, may enter too.

Verse 20 repeats (as in 5:6 and 5:10) the phrase from Psalm 110:4 about the high priest *after the order of Melchizedek*. This introduces the reader to an expanded explanation about Melchizedek and Jesus (Chapter 7).

§ § § § § § §

The Message of Hebrews 6:9-20

This passage is a call to Christians to strive toward the realization of a *hope* that is based on a *promise*. The promise is God's and therefore absolutely sure. That is because God is constant. As in all of Scripture, God is the given. Life, the result of God's creative action, has meaning only as response to God. God makes that response possible in a promise. God makes that promise realizable through Jesus who clears the way and shows the way and leads the way to realizing the hope.

Hope is what distinguishes the Christian message. A life that drifts is hopeless. The implication is plain that even a life of effort, if motivated by the desire for pleasure, position, or power, is a life without hope. Such efforts are self-circled, are limited to existence in the world, and are not drawn toward God. They miss the point of life: access to God.

The message of hope is to Christians who:
§ express Christianity in loving service;
§ are refugees from this world, seeking God.

It is an appeal to Christians to:
§ grow in the hope they live by;
§ avoid sluggishness in Christian living;
§ imitate those who, by faith and patience, have realized God's promise.

It assures Christians that:
§ God will unchangeably carry out the divine purpose and promise to them;
§ Jesus helps us come into God's presence.

It tells Christians they can:
§ seize the hope God has set before them;
§ experience life in God's presence forever.

§ § § § § § §

PART SEVEN Hebrews 7

Introduction to This Chapter

Hebrews 5:9-10 prepares for the fourth and longest lesson about Christ's high priestly action on our behalf. It runs from 6:20, following the warnings and encouragement in 5:11–6:20, to 10:18. Chapter 7 begins the lesson by proving that Jesus is the true, the only, and the needed mediator between human sin and God's righteousness.

The emphasis of the previous paragraph was "hope." Jesus makes the fulfillment of hope possible. Because hope is for access to God, and human sin makes that access to God impossible, Jesus in his sacrifice has cancelled the negating power of sin. In so doing he has made the hope of access to God viable for the sinner. That suggests a priestly function. Jesus was like a high priest, making possible the forgiveness of sins through his priestly act.

High priests, however, had been functioning for centuries as mediators between sinful humankind and a righteous God. Yet people continued to be caught by the clutches of sin. It was necessary to prove that Jesus is more effective because his priesthood is of a higher order. The story of Melchizedek provided the way to prove this fact, by allegory. It proves Jesus to be a greater priest than the Levite priests of the old Israel. As a priest of the new covenant, Jesus replaces the old covenant with a better one. His own sacrifice of himself is eternally effective.

Here is an outline of Hebrews 7.
I. Who Is Melchizedek? (7:1-3)
II. Melchizedek Superior to Old Priesthood (7:4-10)
III. The Levite Priests Were Inadequate (7:11-12)
IV. There Is a Better Order of Priesthood (7:13-17)
V. A Greater Hope Supersedes the Law (7:18-19)
VI. Christ Is Priest of a Better Covenant (7:20-22)
VII. Christ Is Our Eternal High Priest (7:23-25)
VIII. Christ's Sacrifice Is Permanent (7:26-28)

Who Is Melchizedek? (7:1-3)

Hebrews 6:20 is the major argument of Hebrews. Chapter 7 expands on this argument. Who is Melchizedek, and where does he come into the Bible story and the Christian faith?

The story of Melchizedek is found in Genesis 14:18-20. It breaks into the middle of a story of Abraham's meeting with the king of Sodom. Abraham had pursued and defeated five raiding chieftains. He recaptured the booty and people they had taken. On his return from battle the king of Sodom came out to thank him.

The sudden appearance in this setting of Melchizedek, king of Salem, is to remind all readers that credit for Abraham's victory goes to God, not Abraham. Someone greater than Abraham comes, in the name of *God, the Most High*, to bless him. Abraham, in turn, gives Melchizedek *a tenth of everything*.

Some scholars think Melchizedek may have been the name of a king of a little town called Salim. He is usually associated in Hebrew tradition with Jerusalem (called *Salem* in Psalm 76:2), which was a very old city-kingdom long before King David and the Israelites took it to be their capital. *The God Most High* was a frequent title for God among the Hebrews from early times (see Numbers 24:16) and is also found in the psalms.

This chapter is an allegory—a story used for moral instruction, in which actions are used as symbols, and persons are used as types to represent ideas and other persons the storyteller wishes to emphasize. At the time Hebrews was written, allegorical Bible interpretation was a typical and favorite form of teaching among Jewish rabbis.

Verses 1-3 give the setting for the allegory. Melchizedek represents righteousness and peace, because he is *first, by translation of his name, king of righteousness* [justice], and the name of his city, *Salem*, means *peace*.

One element of teaching by allegory was to find meaning even in omissions. Since, for example, the story of Melchizedek fails to mention anything about his birth or death, or about any predecessors or successors, it can be inferred that he never was born, never died, and, having no genealogy, is a perpetual kin of righteousness and peace. On that basis, the writer of Hebrews can say, *resembling the Son of God he continues a priest for ever* [in perpetuity]. *Righteousness* and *peace* would be, in popular anticipation of the coming messiah, characteristics of his kingdom.

Hebrews finds significance, which will be explained later (verse 4), in the fact that Abraham gave, in return, *a tenth part of everything*. It was a custom for a victor in battle to give to his god—hence to the priest of his god—a tenth of the spoils of war as a thank-offering for the god's help in battle. This was not a custom in Israel.

Melchizedek Superior to Old Priesthood (7:4-10)

Levi was one of the twelve sons of the patriarch, Jacob. Jacob was the grandson of Abraham, from whom the people of Israel were descended, according to Genesis. Moses and Aaron belonged to the tribe of Levi. When Moses led the people of Israel out of Egypt, he designated his brother, Aaron, to be high priest. Aaron's descendants continued to hold the high priest's office. The descendants of the tribe of Levi received the prescribed offerings of the people (see Numbers

18:21, 24-26), who were required to give a tenth of their possessions to them for their support and the support of the religious life of the people of Israel.

On the basis of the allegory, the writer of Hebrews argues Melchizedek's superiority. *See how great he is!* Abraham gave him *a tithe of the spoils*—a tenth of *everything* (verse 2). Levites, who are mortals, receive the tenth from their relatives, fellow-descendants of Abraham, by *a commandment in the law* (Numbers 18:21-24). Abraham, not because of any law, but because he recognized the greatness of Melchizedek, gave him a tithe. It was acknowledged in ancient Middle Eastern culture that the greater had the right of a tithe of the lesser people. For example, the Lord warns Israel, through Samuel the prophet, that if they have a king, he will have a right to demand at least a tenth of everything they own (see 1 Samuel 8:10-18). Melchizedek, who is immortal and is not a Levite priest by descent, receives a tenth from Abraham, ancestor of the Levite priests. This signifies, the writer reasons, that the Levite priests were themselves giving their tenth to the priest Melchizedek because they were Abraham's unborn descendants, thus proving that he belonged to a higher priesthood.

The *loins* (verse 9) were looked upon as the seat of physical vitality which contained the posterity of a man (see Genesis 35:11). Melchizedek blessed Abraham, *him who had the promises* (6:13-15). *It is beyond dispute*, Hebrews says, *that the inferior is blessed by the superior*.

The writer of Hebrews has made a case for the superiority of Melchizedek over Abraham, the honored ancestor of the Hebrew people. The author is in no way setting out a new doctrine about a mystical eternal being named Melchizedek. Melchizedek is purely an allegorical symbol used here to illustrate the superiority of Christ over the Levite. That assertion follows in the next paragraph of the Hebrews sermon.

The Levite Priests Were Inadequate (7:11-12)

The thesis of this Hebrews passage is like the earlier one about the need for a more perfect rest. If Joshua had given them rest in the land God had promised them, God would not have had to speak later of a more perfect rest (*speak later of another day*, 4:8). In the same way, Hebrews now says that if the Levite priesthood had been adequate as mediator between the people's sins and God, there would be no need (as there is) for another priest who is like Melchizedek.

The word *perfection* (verse 11) is the word used to describe the rite of priestly consecration in the Hebrew law. Psalm 110:4 speaks of a different kind of priest who, like Melchizedek, does not belong to the tribe of Levite priests. That means, the Hebrews sermon is saying, that a new kind of priest is needed. If a new kind of priest is needed, this is obviously because the consecration (perfection) of the Levite priests is inadequate. This will lead to the conclusion that only Christ, the true high priest, perfect forever, will fill the need (7:28).

It follows, says the writer, that if the Levite priesthood is inadequate, then the law that came through these priests is also inadequate. If the priesthood must be changed, so must the law. The better priesthood, after the order of Melchizedek (in other words, like Melchizedek), will bring with it a better law.

There Is a Better Order of Priesthood (7:13-17)

The other reference to Melchizedek in the Old Testament is in Psalm 110. This psalm addresses the king in Jerusalem, calling him *a priest forever after the order of Melchizedek* (verse 4). The king was not a priest *after the order of Aaron* (Hebrews 7:11). That is, he was not a descendant of the priests designated to serve at the altar in the sanctuary. Nevertheless, in line with ancient cultural practice, he did have a high priestly character in that he represented his people to God. As such, the psalmist says, "You belong to the line of that ancient priest-king of Jerusalem, Melchizedek."

Like Melchizedek, Jesus belonged *to another tribe*. Like the kings in Jerusalem, Jesus, a descendant of King David, was of the tribe of Judah. *It is evident that our Lord was descended from Judah*. This was affirmed by all Christians (see Luke 3:23-33; Romans 1:3). He is a priest, not because of human ancestry, a legal requirement concerning bodily descent like the Levite priests. His qualification is much greater: the power of an indestructible life. The Levite priests, born into Levite families, inherited their priesthood, and eventually died. Their lives were ephemeral. They were imperfect and transient. Jesus, on the other hand, is perfect and indestructible. His priesthood is independent of human regulation and frailty.

A Greater Hope Supersedes the Law (7:18-19)

These verses contrast the failure of the law with the new hope in Christ. On the one hand the Levite priesthood had failed. The law under them failed. It is not that the law was bad, for God sent it. Rather, the law was transitory; as such it was a shadow of a greater hope to come.

The writer has already said that a change of priesthood and law is necessary (see 7:12). Now it is said more directly that the old law, the *former commandment*, is out of date because it never worked anyway. Now, therefore, it is *set aside*. It is replaced by a *better hope*. The old law's *weakness and uselessness* was that it could not secure for people true forgiveness for their sins. Without such forgiveness no sinners could have access to fellowship with God. The law made nothing perfect. The perfection desired is human communion with God. The law could not bring this about.

On the other hand, there is hope. Hope succeeds where law failed. Through hope we draw near to God.

Christ Is Priest of a Better Covenant (7:20-22)

And, the writer adds, there is another reason why Jesus is a greater priest than the Levite priests. Here again the writer uses contrast: On the one hand the Levite priests were never confirmed in their office by an oath. On the other hand, God confirmed Jesus with an oath. The writer again quotes Psalm 110:4. *The LORD has sworn* (has made a vow). A vow made by God has already been mentioned (6:10). God vowed to do what had been promised to Abraham. Since God vowed, nothing could be more certain and unbreakable.

This is what makes the new covenant, of which Jesus is priest forever, a better covenant than the law of the Levites, which was based on the old covenant made through Moses. The new covenant is sure, effective, perfect, unbreakable, and forever. *Covenant* is the crowning thought toward which the writer has been building the whole sermon. Jesus is greater than angels who brought the law to Moses, greater than Moses who mediated the old covenant, and greater than the priests who administered the old covenant. This Jesus is *surety*, that is, he guarantees this new covenant. A covenant is an agreement between two parties. The meaning of the new covenant God gives through Jesus will be discussed by the author of Hebrews in Chapter 9.

Christ Is Our Eternal High Priest (7:23-25)

The series of contrasts continues. On the one hand, *the former priests were many*. They were subject to death. They were temporary priests. They all had to pass their office on to successors. On the other hand, Jesus lives forever. He is a permanent priest. He does not have to pass his office on to successors. The word that the writer uses to express this means, in its etymological sense, *no one could walk beside him*. There is no one worthy enough to whom he could transfer his office. The priesthood is exclusively his because he alone is deathless.

What is the consequence of this role having been given to Jesus? Jesus is always able to save, completely and definitely, those who approach God through him. He is always alive and interceding for them. This intercession for them is not the ritual or pleading of a human priest. Now Jesus is in the presence of God, seated in the position of exclusive honor (8:1, 2). He mediates for the human sinner with the authority God has given him (3:1).

The Hebrews sermon assures Christians. It is a statement of joyous assurance for those who are drawing near to God. They keep moving toward God, who is their goal. They trust in Christ, the perfect ever-alive mediator, the opener of the way to God.

Christ's Sacrifice Is Permanent (7:26-28)

These verses sum up and reinforce what has been said before about the high priesthood of Jesus. There are three qualities of the high priest, Jesus, that make him different.

First, he is *holy, blameless, unstained*. Above all, says the writer, Jesus' character makes the greatest difference. He is holy because God's holiness abhors sin, and Jesus, without sin, is pleasing in a way no creature of God's can be. He is blameless because he has harmed no one. *Blameless* in Greek means *harm-less*, to be completely without the sinner's ego reaction to what others do. Jesus is unstained because he has done no wrong.

Second, he is *separated from sinners*. This does not mean that Jesus will have nothing to do with sinners; his priesthood is for sinners. What it does mean is that Jesus is in a different class from people on earth who sin. Tempted, he did not surrender to sin. He never did that which separates people from God.

Third, he is *exalted above the heavens*. The author and first readers understood the universe as consisting of the earth, what is below the earth, and a series of heavens above the earth. Jesus, says the author, is above all of this. He cannot be located even in a heaven, because he is with God. Thus, he is above all that mortal beings can imagine.

Verse 27 is another contrast. Human priests offered animal sacrifices as an appeal to God to forgive the sins of the people. In so doing, they had to use the sacrifice for their own sins as well, because they were all sinners (5:3). The law describes the sacrifice Aaron, the first high priest, made for his own sins (Leviticus 16:6-11). Jesus did not have to sacrifice for his sins. He had no sin. Nothing separated him from God.

As sinless high priest, Jesus made one sacrifice: himself. The words that describe Jesus as a fitting high priest in verse 26 are words which were also used to describe an acceptable sacrifice: *holy* (pleasing to God), *blameless* (unblemished), *unstained* (undefiled). The prescribed sacrifice, held once a year to cover the previous year's sins (Leviticus 16), was called "making atonement," making the people at one with God after the separation caused by their sins. Sin offerings were sacrificed throughout the year, however, (Leviticus 4), and were performed by priests who, themselves, were sinners. So Hebrews says they must offer sacrifices daily for their own as well as other people's sins. Because Jesus was both the sacrificer and the sacrificed, and so was sinless, his sacrifice did not need to be repeated. It was offered *once for all*.

Verse 28 repeats the double distinction that, in contrast to priests appointed in all their human weakness and without a confirming oath, Jesus, as a Son, is appointed by God. God confirms Jesus' appointment with *the word of the oath*, that is, with a promise made with a vow (see the comments on *vow* and *oath* above in verses 20-21).

Finally, Jesus is the greater high priest because he *has been made perfect forever*. Jesus has accomplished that which God had intended. God's intention was to make possible communion between sinners and God. God's holiness can never be adulterated with sin. It can never be permissive of sin. Sin can never stand in the presence of God because, by definition, sin is rebellion against God's righteousness, and thus separation from God. God appointed a Son (described in Chapter 1), who alone was able, once for all, to make possible complete atonement with God. Hebrews implies that Jesus could have failed. He could have come through his human experience unholy, blemished, and stained. If he had failed, humanity would never have found access to God's presence. God would never have had fellowship with humankind. The Son, Jesus, did not fail. He carried through God's intentions (as described in 2:9-18). His perfection forever was what Jesus' obedience did in God's behalf for humanity.

§ § § § § § §

The Message of Hebrews 7

This chapter's message is based on four assumptions:
§ God desires communion with human beings.
§ Human beings desire to draw near to God, without whom life will never be fulfilled.
§ Nevertheless sin, which is rebellion against God's righteousness, separates human beings from God.
§ Attempts to break down the barrier of sin and to find access to God have failed.
These attempts have failed because:
§ they are devised by a human system;
§ they are conducted by human beings;
§ these persons are not confirmed in their work by God;
§ they are limited by weakness, sin, and death.
However, Jesus Christ is a mediator between our sinful lives and God because:
§ he is independent of human limitations;
§ through suffering obedience to God he has been made perfect forever, holy, blameless, unstained by sin, having successfully resisted temptation.
From now on there is no need for any other atonement. Jesus Christ has done it all, what no one else could do.
On these bases, Hebrews assures the Christians that, though human systems and devices fail, those who draw near to God can know that Christ is always there as our mediator making access to God forever possible.

§ § § § § § §

PART EIGHT Hebrews 8:1–9:14

Introduction to These Chapters

This passage describes the new covenant between God and humanity which Jesus, the true high priest, guarantees. It seeks to show that the human institutions of Hebrew religion were a copy, or shadow, of the reality in heaven. Jesus is the true high priest in the true sanctuary.

Here is an outline of this passage.
I. High Priest in the True Sanctuary (8:1-2)
II. Jesus Is Not in an Earthly Sanctuary (8:3-5)
III. High Priest of a Better Covenant (8:6-13)
IV. The First Covenant Had Earthly Rules (9:1-5)
V. Rituals of the Earthly Sanctuary (9:6-10)
VI. Jesus, the One Effective Sacrifice (9:11-14)

High Priest in the True Sanctuary (8:1-2)

Typical of the Hebrews sermon is a concluding repetition of what has been said, as in Chapter 8:1, with a new idea added, as in 8:2. *This is the point in what we are saying, the gist of it, the essence of it,* or, as the King James Version translates it, *this is the sum.* It is, indeed, the main assurance that we have such a high priest.

Seated at the right hand repeats the quotation from Psalm 110:1 and reminds the reader of Jesus' position of honor, and his closeness to God, *the Majesty,* literally, *the Greatness.* God is so great and holy that devout Jews would not take God's name on their lips. They spoke of God by an attribute such as greatness. *In heaven* means literally *in the heavens*. As the heavens are above and beyond the earth, so is God.

The new idea, although suggested before in Hebrews, comes with the phrase *the true tent*. The tent refers to the collapsible tent sanctuary which Exodus 25–31 describes as being constructed so that it could be moved along with the people of Israel when they were wandering from place to place in the desert (Exodus 33:7). This tent was set up by human beings. *The true tent*, the real sanctuary of God, is not set up by humans but by the Lord. It is in this true tent sanctuary, eternal and in heaven (with God), where Jesus is *minister*. The word for *minister* is a technical one of a priest carrying out the functions of worship. It is transliterated in modern church worship as *liturgist*.

Well known in Greek writings was the concept that everything on earth is a copy or shadow of a heavenly reality on which it is patterned. This concept, older than the philosophical school of Plato that developed it, is that the visible world is a reflection of a real but invisible world. As shadows come and go and are often distorted, so the material copies of the spiritual world are temporary and less than perfect.

Jesus Is Not in an Earthly Sanctuary (8:3-5)

Earthly high priests in an earthly sanctuary must make ritual sacrifices and sin offerings in behalf of the people, in accordance with the law. The writer has already pointed this out (5:1) and will expand on it later (9:6). At present, the writer wants to make clear that these high priests serve copies of the real sanctuary where Jesus serves. Jesus is not an earthly priest. He was not a Levite serving in a sanctuary made of perishable material by human hands.

Nevertheless, it is necessary for this priest also to have something to offer. Otherwise, he would not be a priest, since it is a priest's function to make a sacrifice for the people. Who is *this priest*, and what will he offer? The author has Jesus in mind, and his offering of the perfect and unrepeatable offering of himself. This also has been mentioned before (7:27). The author will later speak of it more fully in contrast with earthly priests (9:11-12), at which point he will name the heavenly high priest, Christ. Here he prepares for this revelation by simply saying that this priest is not an earthly priest. If he were on earth he would not be a priest at all, because the only sacrifices made in the earthly sanctuary are those prescribed by law, and there are already priests for this function. Thus, the author prepares the readers for Jesus' different kind of priesthood in a different kind of sanctuary where he will make a different kind of offering (9:24-26). In the meantime, however, the writer emphasizes that *they* (the Levite priests) and their functions and the sanctuary in which they serve are only a copy and shadow. The heavenly sanctuary is the real sanctuary where Jesus serves (8:2). The writer quotes Exodus 25:40, that when Moses was on the mountain receiving the law from God, God showed him a pattern for the tent sanctuary he was to build. The writer of Hebrews may have read a book about the life of Moses written by his early contemporary, Philo. Philo quotes this verse and explains that Moses saw the plan of the heavenly sanctuary itself, and built the earthly tent of meeting to be like the one he saw. His was only a copy.

High Priest of a Better Covenant (8:6-13)

Quoting from the Book of Jeremiah in the Old Testament, Hebrews sets forth what lies at the heart of Christian belief: the *new covenant*. The covenant was an experience of communion with God made possible by the graciousness of God, and sealed by a sacrificial ceremony.

The beginning of verse 6 corresponds to the beginning of verse 4 where we read: *Now if he were on earth . . . .* But he wasn't a priest on earth. *But,* we now read, *as it is*, he has his ministry in the heavens. The author still refrains from mentioning the name of this priest. *Christ* does not appear in the original Greek text, but is inserted by the translator so that the English-speaking reader will understand of whom Hebrews is writing. The reader of the Greek sermon is kept in suspense.

Christ's *ministry* (the same word as in verse 2) is that he *mediates* this new covenant. The word *mediate* generally meant to arbitrate as an intermediary in a civil transaction. Moses was spoken of as mediator of the covenant. Hebrews always uses the term for Christ's action, his life and suffering in mediating between our sin and God's holiness. Thus, Christ clears the way for us to approach God's presence. He has made the human-divine relationship possible.

If the old covenant had succeeded in doing this mediating, there would have been no need for a new covenant (verse 7). Hebrews repeats the formula: The need for a new and better (rest, 4:8; priesthood, 7:11; covenant, 8:7) is due to the failure of the old and weaker.

What Christ does is to supply the deficiency of the old earthly covenant with the new covenant promised long before through Jeremiah. It is a better covenant based on better promises which give a firmer foundation for hope than did the weak priesthood and the ineffective law which underlay the old covenant (see Hebrews 7:12, 18-19). These better promises are those spoken by God (as the writer of Hebrews would say) in Jeremiah 31:31-34, the longest Old Testament quotation in the New Testament. The better promises are: (1) The new covenant will be internalized. It will enter into their minds and be in their understanding, affecting their attitudes and disposition. It will be on their hearts, at the center of their conscience as a motivational force (verse 10). (2) It will make for a genuine relationship between God and people (*for all shall know me*, verse 11). (3) It will pardon (*I will remember their sins no more*, verse 12). The quotation in

Hebrews does not correspond word for word with what we find in the Book of Jeremiah. That is because our English translation is from the Hebrew text. The writer of Hebrews is quoting what he remembers from the popular Greek translation of his time.

The First Covenant Had Earthly Rules (9:1-5)

The Hebrews sermon continues to discuss the themes of sacrifice and forgiveness. These verses describe the worship of God in the earthly sanctuary and in its *Holy of Holies*, the setting of the old covenant.

Now Hebrews goes on to explain what was wrong with the first covenant. It was dependent on regulated forms of worship and an earthly sanctuary. The giving, accepting, and institution of the first covenant is detailed in Exodus 24. This is followed in Exodus by a description of the tent of worship. The writer of Hebrews sees this as indication that the earthly worship sanctuary is essential to the keeping of the old covenant. The sanctuary housed the tablets on which the covenant was engraved. The covenant took the place in the sanctuary of the statue of a god in non-Jewish temples.

The sanctuary is now described. There were two rooms or tents. The outer, larger room was called the *Holy Place*. Only the priests could enter it. It was furnished with a lampstand and a table for utensils and bread. The lampstand stood by the south wall. It was made of gold and had seven branches. The table of gold-covered acacia wood stood by the north wall. It held utensils used in ritual ceremonies (see Exodus 25:23-30) and the bread of the Presence, twelve small cakes placed fresh on the table every sabbath. It was called bread of the Presence because it was near God's Presence Chamber (described in verses 3-6).

At the end of the room hung an embroidered linen curtain (Exodus 26:31-33). This second curtain (the first curtain hung at the entrance of the Holy Place) separated the smaller, inner room or tent at the west end of the sanctuary. This room was a cube, being of the same width, depth, and height. It was called the Holy of Holies. No one was allowed to enter this holy room except the high priest, and he could enter only once a year. Hebrews mentions two pieces of furniture here: the golden altar of incense and the ark of the covenant. According to the plan in Exodus 30:1-6, the incense altar stood in the outer room near the curtain. Incense was burned on this altar. The writer of Hebrews may have been thinking of the burning of incense in the Holy of Holies, required of the high priest when he entered it (Leviticus 16:12). The altar was a square table of acacia wood covered with gold and with projecting horns. The blood of sin-offerings was sprinkled on these horns on the Day of Atonement, once a year.

The ark of the covenant was a gold-plated box of acacia wood. Two stone tablets engraved with the covenant (Exodus 25:16) were kept in it. The writer of Hebrews understood that the box was also supposed to contain a golden urn holding the manna (Exodus 16:33-34), the food which the Israelites miraculously found during their desert crossing (Exodus 16). It also contained Aaron's rod, the rod of the high priest which was said to have sprouted buds, blossoms, and ripe almonds (Numbers 17:8-11).

On the ark was a slab of gold called the mercy seat (Exodus 25:17-22). This was the nearest the Hebrews came to locating God, and that only temporarily. Israel's God was said to *appear in the cloud* (Exodus 25:22; Leviticus 16:2) on the Day of Atonement when the high priest entered the Holy of Holies with the blood of the bull sacrificed as a sin offering (Leviticus 16:14). Above the mercy seat were hung the cherubim of glory. These were two gold figures of mixed features so they would not resemble any actual animal, in accordance with the second commandment. (Ezekiel, too, had a vivid dream of them; see Ezekiel 10.) They had wings overshadowing the mercy seat. The glory was the radiant presence of God among the people.

The writer could go on and on (verse 5), for the descriptions in Exodus and Leviticus are detailed. But it was more important to turn to the significance of this earthly sanctuary and of the Day of Atonement.

Rituals of the Earthly Sanctuary (9:6-10)

Hebrews has described the earthly sanctuary, drawing details from Exodus, Numbers, and Leviticus. Now the author proceeds to describe rituals. In describing them, the author is telling a parable with double meaning. First, the priests must continually be going about their ritual duties in the outer tent, the Holy Place. This represents the first human experience of worship. It is the copy of true worship. Second, only once a year the high priest goes into the second room, the inner tent. Even once a year he would not dare to go without the blood of the sin-offering, which he sprinkles on and before the mercy seat (Leviticus 16:14-16) as a means of asking God to restore relationship with the people. The true second room or inner tent, the real heavenly Holy of Holies, has not really been entered yet.

This the Holy Spirit indicates: That is, says Hebrews, if you read God's word as inspired by the Holy Spirit, you can understand its deeper, mystical meaning. The deeper meaning is that the first, earthly ritual does not give access to the true Holy of Holies where God really dwells. The second or inner room which is the true, heavenly Holy of Holies cannot be entered so long as the first one stands. This is subjective. It applies to persons, not to Christ who has already entered the true Holy of Holies (verse 11). Clearly, as long as you depend on and remain in the sanctuary of the old covenant, there is no open access into God's presence.

Verse 9 says that the first tent, the earthly sanctuary, is

provisional (*symbolic*) for our times. It is only a transitory foreshadowing of the eternal, heavenly sanctuary.

All these arrangements are as ineffective and temporary as the old covenant they support. They are regulations for the body, associated with the sentient and external life, and cannot get the worshipers into the true presence of God. The *body* (verse 10) and *conscience* (verse 9) are contrasted. This is an appeal to move from a religion of formal practice to an inner faith affecting the personal, moral, and spiritual life of the believer. The sin-offering is only an external rite. It does not really affect the conscience, the sin-consciousness of worshipers. The establishment of the new covenant will change all this.

Jesus, the One Effective Sacrifice (9:11-14)

These verses conclude the descriptions of sanctuary and sacrifice. They tell what Christ did, and the significance of what he did.

The time of reformation (verse 10) is now here, because Christ appeared. *The good things that have come* (or, preferably, *are about to come*, 10:1) is a way of saying that the good things of the age of promise, the time of consummation, are already here. The Son has come, and he did for us what no one else could do. As high priest, he entered the Holy of Holies in the heavenly sanctuary, which is not of this creation, not humanly devised. He sacrificed his own blood and truly, not just ritually, cleansed our consciences of sin.

It was the blood of the slaughtered animals (not the dead animals) that the high priest brought into the Holy of Holies. It did not do any good. The point, however, is that the high priest was offering the sacrificed life of the animals. Jesus, bringing his blood into the heavenly sanctuary, brought his life, sacrificed for all. It was his life of complete obedience to God's will, thus securing an eternal redemption. He will not have to do it again. It was because *he learned obedience through what he suffered* (5:8) that he was made *perfect through suffering* (2:10).

The significance of what he did is that, by his act, Christ saves us from dead works to a living God. Christ is our redemption.

§ § § § § § §

The Message of Hebrews 8:1–9:14

The great assurance in the Christian life is Jesus. This section of the Hebrews sermon emphasizes the ministry of Jesus as high priest. Jesus serves in a heavenly sanctuary, far more real than an earthly copy of it. Jesus made possible a new covenant, far more effective than the old law and covenant. Jesus made a sacrifice of himself once for all, which makes possible our approach to God, a possibility the old sacrifices of the Hebrew sanctuary did not fulfill.

The passage in Hebrews assumes that our greatest goal in life is fellowship with God. Our religion does not bring about fellowship with God if:

§ we think of Jesus as a teacher of an earthly religion, no matter how fine it is;

§ we try to live by a code of conduct, based on human rules, regulation, and rites, no matter how excellent.

Our faith will arrive at fellowship with God eternally if:

§ we trust in Jesus as God's appointed;

§ we understand Jesus as our high priest interceding for us in God's presence;

§ we accept in our minds and hearts God's will for us as demonstrated in the life and death of Jesus;

§ we accept God's full, free pardon of our sins;

§ we accept Christ's suffering in our behalf to purify our conscience so that we can serve the living God.

§ § § § § § §

PART NINE: Hebrews 9:15–10:18

Introduction to These Chapters

This is the final section on the high priesthood of Jesus. It goes into greater detail to show how Christ's sacrifice, in contrast to the old and ineffective sacrifices, is the means by which the new covenant God promised is made to work. By his sacrifice we are forgiven and purified forever.

Here is an outline of this passage.
 I. The New Covenant Becomes Effective (9:15-17)
 II. Old Covenant Sealed by Blood Sacrifice (9:18-22)
 III. Christ Mediates the New Covenant (9:23-26)
 IV. Jesus Receives Those Who Repent (9:27-28)
 V. Old Sacrifices Were Repeated (10:1-4)
 VI. Christ Replaced the Old Sacrifices (10:5-10)
 VII. Christ Has Purified His People (10:11-14)
 VIII. The New Covenant of God's Grace (10:15-18)

The New Covenant Becomes Effective (9:15-17)

Christ is mediator of a new covenant. He is the one who arranges the new covenant. As mediator, Christ is at the same time (1) the high priest making an offering for the sins of the people, (2) the offering itself, (3) the testator making a will, (4) the executor seeing that the will is executed, and (5) the guarantor for the will, making sure that its benefits are distributed to all the people.

Through the analogy of a will, Hebrews shows that God's promised new covenant could only take effect upon Christ's death. That is another way of saying that it took Christ's death to redeem us from our failure to keep the old covenant.

The Greek word used for *covenant* between God and us also means, in common Greek usage, a will or testament in which a testator determines the disposition of his property after his death. Hebrews makes use of this double meaning of the word. (See also Galatians 3:15-17.) The analogy of a will makes two points. The first is to explain how it is that the promise of a new covenant made hundreds of years before had only now come into effect. As a will takes effect only on the death of the testator who made it, so the promised new covenant could take effect only on the death of Christ. The second point is that, the death having taken place, the covenant is put into effect for the beneficiaries.

The beneficiaries of the will are *those who are called* (verse 15). The author of Hebrews has to deal with the same problem faced by Paul. Surely this great offer of God's must be for all. Nevertheless, obviously not all persons express a desire for it, or seek it, or receive it. Hence, the phrase *the ones who have been called*. They are the people of God, who keep faith with God. The promised eternal inheritance is the benefit past generations of God's people have hoped for. Only now, through Christ's death, can they receive it. Now they are freed from their sins. The transgressions under the first covenant were the limitations which the old covenant could not overcome and which prevented hopeful believers from receiving the full experience of forgiveness.

Old Covenant Sealed by Blood Sacrifice (9:18-22)

In Hebrews, blood, death, and covenant are all related. In these verses the author tells why *blood* is such an important symbol. From earliest times, blood, the principle of life, has been considered to have a mystic potency. The author of Hebrews notes the comparative ineffectiveness of blood in the rites of purification, expiation, and atonement ceremonies of ancient Israel. That does not mean there is no power in the blood. It means only that no blood could be so effectively powerful as that of Christ who comes from and is with God.

What *had been declared by Moses* (verse 19) is taken from Exodus 24:3-8. The ceremony involving sprinkling of blood is taken from Leviticus 14:4-7 and Numbers 19:1-6. The writer of Hebrews adds that the blood was mixed with water to dilute the blood. Both blood and water are, to the author of Hebrews, symbols of cleansing. The *hyssop* was probably a small wall plant. Its branches were tied together with wool that had been dyed red. This was used as a sprinkler. The phrase *blood of the covenant* is used by Moses (Exodus 24:8) when he inaugurates the covenant between God and the people of Israel. The sprinkling of blood is interpreted as a ceremony for making the people clean.

The author has used death in two illustrations. One, the death of him who makes the will, is necessary for the will to come into effect. Two, the sacrifice, in which the life blood is spilled, makes clean those for whom the sacrifice is made. It atones for their sins. In both cases, the writer is saying that the sacrificial death of Christ makes operative God's forgiveness of the sinner. The author will expand this idea in the following verses.

Christ Mediates the New Covenant (9:23-26)

All these sacrificial ceremonies that took place in front of the tent of meeting, the earthly sanctuary, were copies of the real thing. Here is the scheme in this passage:
(a) The earthly sanctuary, the tent of meeting in Israel, made with hands, is a copy of the heavenly sanctuary where God is always present.
(b) The earthly high priest, repeating the ritual of purification annually, is a copy of Jesus Christ, the true high priest. He appears in the presence of God on our

behalf, making the sacrifice for forgiveness of sins just once for all time.

(c) The sacrifice of animals and the sprinkling of their blood by the high priest is a copy of Jesus' sacrifice of himself, by his own blood to put away sin.

By his death, Christ has consecrated the new covenant and the heavenly sanctuary. As the true high priest, he has done this in the presence of God on our behalf. The earthly high priest once a year carried the blood of the sacrificial victim into the Holy of Holies where God was present. The true high priest, Jesus, enters the Holy of Holies where God is truly present, bringing his own blood. Thus he has removed the people's sins.

Christ did not need to offer himself repeatedly, as the high priest (on earth). People have always needed repeated sacrifices, experiences of forgiveness, because people are repeatedly sinning. However, Christ's sacrifice is perfect and unrepeatable. It is for the past (verse 15) and for always.

There are two ages in Jewish-Christian thinking: this present age (*But as it is*, verse 26) and the age to come. This present age is a time in which God is active and in charge, but there is also much evil—rebellion against God—which is sin. God's plan is to supersede this present age with the age to come. The age to come is to be brought in by God's messiah. The new age will be a perfect age of righteousness under God's complete rule.

What Jesus has done by coming to earth has been to initiate the new covenant *at the end of the age* (of this present age). Hebrews represents the view of all first-century Christians that Christ's coming is the culmination of present history.

Jesus Receives Those Who Repent (9:27-28)

Speaking about Jesus' coming as high priest (verse 11) *at the end of the age to put away sin by the sacrifice of himself* (verse 26) leads the writer to speak of Jesus' imminent return to usher in the new age to come. The good things to come have been in mind throughout this sermon (2:5; 6:5; 9:11; see the comments on 9:11 and 10:1).

Jesus' self-sacrifice once for all at the end of the age is not to be interpreted to mean that he will not come again. And his coming again is not to be interpreted as a repeat event of his sacrifice to deal with sin. That has been done. Death comes once to all, and Christ has already died once for all to bear the sins of many.

Death is not the end. Even human beings, after they die, face judgment. And Jesus, having died a sacrificial death, will return. He will return this time for those who have not given up and who are eagerly waiting for him.

Judgment is set over against salvation. God, the judge (12:23), has offered salvation in Christ. As the writer has already said (6:4) and will say again (10:26-27), those who reject Christ's sacrifice for them reject the hope of salvation. *Judgment* is a bleak word for them. The contrast is between them and the happy ones who have accepted Christ's sacrifice in their behalf and have remained faithful. They now await his return with eagerness. Salvation is theirs. Their hope will be fulfilled on Christ's return. The verb used here (*waiting*, watching) characterizes earliest Christianity as an expectant people.

Old Sacrifices Were Repeated (10:1-4)

The *law* Hebrews refers to is the regulatory system associated with the functions of the levitical priesthood. Those regulations served a purpose in that they reflected the good things God has planned for humanity. Those good things are symbolized by the true and perfect covenant which means the real experience of total forgiveness. Total forgiveness is an opening up of direct relationship with God. The law, as Hebrews has already pointed out (7:18-19), cannot do that good thing. It is only a reflection of that which can. It is like a shadow that has no life in itself. These sacrifices practiced according to the law have no power in themselves to cleanse the worshipers from the consciousness of sin. They are the sacrifices of animals, and it is foolish to suppose that animal blood can clean the conscience. This is the third "impossible" in Hebrews. It is impossible to restore those who have experienced, then denied, the faith (6:4). It is impossible for God not to fulfill the promise (6:18). It is impossible that the blood of bulls and goats should take away sins (10:4).

These sacrifices are only an imitation. Because they do not work, the worshipers try them again and again in a vain attempt to get free from the sin that blocks their consciousness of God. Again, Hebrews repeats the formula with an *if* (see the comments on 4:8; 7:11; and 8:7). *If the worshipers had once been cleansed* . . . But they were not. The sacrifices did not work. All they could do was to remind the worshipers of the sin they could not be rid of.

Christ Replaced the Old Sacrifices (10:5-10)

Christ's sacrifice replaces the law-prescribed sacrifices. Christ's sacrifice is able to purify us because it is made in obedience to God's will. Animals have no consciousness of why they are sacrificed, so of course their sacrifice does no good. Consequently, to fulfill God's promise of fellowship with human creatures, Christ, consciously obedient to that purpose, offered himself. This is the reality of which the earthly sacrifices were but a shadow. The shadow was stated in ritual; the reality is stated in righteousness. Doing God's will is more acceptable to God than animal sacrifices.

The writer to the Hebrews finds this idea in Psalm 40:6-8. The quotation, *but a body hast thou prepared for me,* is different from the same line in our English translation of Psalm 40:6: *But thou has given me an open ear.* That is because the English translation is from the Hebrew text agreed on by ancient Hebrew scholars. The writer to the

Hebrews had an old Greek translation where somehow *ear* was replaced with *body*, two words which could easily be mistaken in hastily written Greek.

The Hebrew psalm says, *God has given me an open ear* to understand God's desire. Hebrews reads this as our Lord, in obedience to God, saying *I have come* (in the incarnate body given me) *to do thy will*. The essential meaning of the psalm, however, is not changed. It is not sacrifices and offerings that God has desired, nor burnt offerings and sin-offerings, but that God's will be done.

The gift of God, given by Christ for us, is what sanctifies us. It consecrates us so that not only Christ, but we, like the high priest, can come into the presence of God. Christ gave his body as a sacrifice to make it possible for us to understand and accept and experience communion with God, which is the divine will.

The phrase, *in the roll of the book*, in the psalm, refers to the code of the law as found in Deuteronomy. The writer of Hebrews expands it to mean that the entire word of God in the (Old Testament) Scriptures speaks of Christ and prepares for his coming.

Christ Has Purified His People (10:11-14)

Christ completely obeyed God's will. He made a thorough sacrifice of himself. God accepted his offering entirely. The task finished, he is seated at the right hand of God. The writer indirectly quotes Psalm 110 again, which had been used earlier in the sermon. This psalm, a blessing on the ideal king of Judah, was interpreted as a reference to the power and glory of the messiah. Jesus quoted it (Mark 12:36). The writer does not discuss *his enemies*. The emphasis here is on the fact that, having finished his offering *for all time*, Christ can sit and wait *at the right hand of God*. Unlike the earthly priests, he can sit on a throne of greatest honor, closest to God.

This place is contrasted with the earthly Aaronic priests. They are always standing, never getting to sit down because their ministry is never finished. They offer the same sacrifices repeatedly. They have to keep on repeating these sin offerings, which can never take away sins. Only Christ is effective as the perfect mediator in our behalf (8:6), the perfect interceder for us (7:25).

By this one sacrifice, Christ perfected for all time those who are consecrated. Christ has made sanctification possible. These words repeat (verse 10) that those who accept Christ's sacrifice and God's forgiveness are thereby made holy in that they are made acceptable in God's holy presence. The Greek uses the present tense, *those who are being made holy*, in its progressive significance because salvation is ongoing. It is a movement toward God.

The New Covenant of God's Grace (10:15-18)

The writer returns to his quotation of Jeremiah 31:31-34 (quoted before in 8:8-12) about the new covenant. Because this is in the word of God, the writer quotes it as the Holy Spirit's witness (see 3:7). The writer uses this quotation as a conclusion to the argument that Christ, in obedience to God's will, has completed for all time the sacrifice that perfects us. The conclusion is: God has forgiven the sins of those who accept Christ's sacrifice (verse 18); God *will remember their sins and their misdeeds no more* (verse 17); God has put laws *on their hearts* and has written them *on their minds*, so that they, like Christ, and by God's grace, will be obedient to God (verse 16). Therefore, all sins having been forgiven and forgotten, there is no need for *any offering for sin*. Forgiveness of sins never means that the sins are excused, but that the sinner's guilt is cancelled. In Hebrews it means even more: that the power of sin to hinder the life of faith is destroyed so that the forgiven is free from the desire to sin and moves forward in faith.

Jesus has brought the new covenant into effect. It is a new era in which the believer, never more sinning against God, has communion forever with God.

§ § § § § § §

The Message of Hebrews 9:15–10:18

This passage is about the new covenant. The old covenant between God and the Hebrew people was inaugurated by the shedding of blood of an animal sacrifice. Because the people kept breaking the covenant, animal sacrifices needed to be repeated annually to restore their relationship with God.

Then Christ came to earth in obedience to God's will for a lasting relationship with humanity. Christ gave his life as a once-for-all sacrifice for people's sins. Having done so, he remains beside God, but will return again to receive the believers who wait for him. Those who wait are they who, released from the power of sin, are called to receive the promised inheritance.

§ This passage tells us that we, too, have received God's call and have received God's promise of eternal fellowship with God, and can be rid of the sins that obstruct our relationship with God.

§ The passage says that we cannot be rid of our sins if we ask forgiveness over and over again, each time only to go back to sinning, if we merely outwardly observe church rites and practices, if we count on persons in ministry (clergy, religious leaders, others) to live Christian lives for us. They too are sinners.

§ This passage tells us that we can be forever rid of our transgressions against God if we come to Christ eager for communion with God; if we accept the offering of Christ's life and death in our behalf; if we trust Christ as our Redeemer; if we obey God's will for our lives; if we allow God to put in our hearts and minds the law of the new covenant; that is, that we will to live by God's will for fellowship with us.

§ § § § § § §

PART TEN Hebrews 10:19-39

Introduction to These Verses

Draw near to God. That is the subject of the sermon. This passage is a call to true worship and faithful endurance. It is the fourth counsel and warning section in the sermon.

The writer of Hebrews has presented Jesus Christ as a high priest mediating on our behalf. He has explained the new covenant as the promise of an undimmed, eternal relationship with God, hope open to all. Now, with the words *Therefore, brethren,* that is, *fellow Christians* (verse 19), the writer turns to encourage readers to draw near to God with faith. A warning is added about the hopelessness for those who disregard and reject Christ's sacrifice for them.

Here is an outline of Hebrews 10:19-39.
I. Jesus Has Opened the Way to God (10:19-21)
II. Let Us Draw Near With Faith (10:22-23)
III. Let Us Encourage One Another (10:24-25)
IV. Do Not Spurn Christ's Sacrifice (10:26-31)
V. Recall Faith Experiences (10:32-34)
VI. Persevere With Confidence (10:35-39)

Jesus Has Opened the Way to God (10:19-21)

These lines assure the readers that they have access to God. The imagery is of the heavenly sanctuary. We are in the Holy Place. We would never be there if it were not for our desire to approach nearer to God. Following Jesus, who has represented us before God, we have come to the place reserved for those consecrated to God. At one end of the room hangs a thick curtain. Beyond it, we know, is the Holy of Holies where God is to be met. Jesus, our great priest over the house of God, goes up to the curtain and opens it. We can see into the room. We can see the mercy seat.

The phrase *he opened for us* (he dedicated, or, especially here, he initiated for us) is the same Greek expression used by Hebrews for Moses' initiation of the old covenant by blood (see 9:18, where the Revised Standard Version has the word *ratified*). This entry into the true Holy of Holies Jesus initiated by his blood. Now at Jesus' invitation we rush eagerly forward, overwhelmed with joy, into the Presence. Or, at least, we can. The way is opened (see 4:14-16; 6:19-20).

Actually, how did Jesus clear the way for us? By the historical act of his self-giving, *by the blood* of Jesus which he brought into God's presence *through his flesh*, through the living Christ who makes continual intercession for us (see 7:25). The way to God is the new and living way (as in John 14:6). This contrasts with the old dead ways we have tried in vain. Christ's flesh becomes the figure for the opening into God's presence. The author may have been suggesting that Jesus' flesh was torn open so the life blood flowed out (*through his flesh*, verse 21). In Mark we read that at the moment of Jesus' death *the curtain of the temple was torn in two, from top to bottom* (Mark 15:38). This was symbolic of the breaking down of the separation between God and us. We no longer have to hide away because of our sin; we are no longer afraid to approach God. We can have confidence to enter the sanctuary. This assurance, or boldness, here signifies the confident trust that comes with unflinching attachment to God. Our longing for God can now find expression in our unhesitating approach to God, because we approach with our high priest, Jesus Christ, whose sacrifice made possible the fulfillment of our need and hope.

Let Us Draw Near With Faith (10:22-23)

The advice in these verses is based on the assurance of verses 19-21. Using the first person plural, the writer urges three "let us" actions: Let us (1) draw near to God (verse 22); (2) hold fast the confession of our hope (verse 23); (3) consider how to stir up one another to love and good works (verse 24).

Now that we have access through what Jesus has done for us, we are urged (as in 4:14-16) to draw near to God. The way is open, but we must ourselves move in it (see Colossians 3:1). *With a true heart* is straightforwardly, wholeheartedly (as in Isaiah 38:3), sincerely, in full assurance of faith (and hope, as in 6:11). This attitude produces a good life. Faith and hope are congruent aspects of the Christian life. The true heart is sprinkled clean from an evil conscience. The conscience is purified by its devotion to the self-giving Christ.

The bodies washed with pure water may refer to water baptism. Sprinkling with blood and sprinkling and washing with water were part of the ritual in the earthly sanctuary and symbolic of being cleansed spiritually (Ezekiel 36:25). Here they symbolize the total consecration of the Christian life, pure body as well as a pure conscience.

The next admonition is very strong: to hold fast, without wavering, unyieldingly. *The confession of our hope* is the profession of our faith, a forward-looking hope in God's unchangeable promises through Jesus Christ. It must not be compromised in any way. *He who promised is faithful.* The faithfulness of God who promised is a major assurance in Hebrews (6:17; 11:11). This reiterates 3:6: *Christ was faithful over God's house as a Son. And we are his house if we hold fast our confidence and pride in our hope.*

Let Us Encourage One Another (10:24-25)

The hope, the faith, the drawing near to God in the one sanctuary, through the one Christ, has essential implications for Christian fellowship. Christianity is not a mysticism in which each of us, without regard to others, seeks our own salvation. It is a group religion. Concern for one another is a part of our approaching God together. We are to stir up one another to love and good works. In 3:13 the writer has asked Christians to counsel and encourage one another. Here, they are urged to incite one another in a ferment of love, which naturally expresses itself in good deeds.

Perhaps this mutual love was lacking in the congregation to whom the sermon was directed. For whatever reason, whether because of lack of harmony in the congregation, or from pressure by non-believers, or from sheer indifference, some were in the habit of neglecting to meet together, missing the assembling of Christians.

Instead, they should encourage one another, especially because (the writer has no doubt) the day of judgment is near. The *Day* is capitalized in the English text because it was a kind of code word among early Christians. It was the Day of the Lord (see 1 Thessalonians 5:4). The meaning of the word came from its usage among the Jews since the time of the prophet Ezekiel (sixth century B.C.), although Jeremiah, too, had used it. The Day is the coming Day when this age will be consummated and the peoples of this age judged. The past will be cleared away. The new Day will dawn. Christians are to live in readiness for its coming.

Do Not Spurn Christ's Sacrifice (10:26-31)

In the light of the *the Day drawing near* (verse 25) with its judgment, these verses are a warning. With encouragement goes warning (2:1-4; 6:4-6). Now that the supremacy of Christ has been established, the meaning of his sacrifice explained, let readers be warned of the risk of rejecting Christ's sacrifice, since it alone is the way to freedom from sin and approach to God. No other sacrifice will help them. Rejecting Christ is self-rejection in the face of judgment.

What is the logic of this assertion? If Christ made one, all-sufficient, unrepeatable sacrifice, what happens to one who has accepted redemption from sin and then returned to sin? There no longer remains a sacrifice for sins. All hope is gone. Such a fearful prospect of judgment has been a terror to many. Early Christians tended to put off baptism until just before death, supposing that the baptismal ceremony would be the sacrament accepting Christ's forgiveness of sins for the first and last time.

The passage deserves careful examination. According to Hebrews, those in trouble here are they who after receiving (positively confessing with understanding of what one is receiving) full knowledge of the truth (which the author has just explained in 10:1-18) about Christ's once-for-all sacrifice for our sins, nevertheless sin deliberately. The phrase is conditional, *if we sin*. *Deliberately* describes an action that consciously violates the offer of Christ. The word could be translated also as *willfully, willingly, intentionally, without compulsion*. A mistake, an unintentional lapse or backsliding, perhaps even a succumbing to a compulsive temptation, are not in this category. Conversely, a willful disdain of and rejection of Christ's sacrifice are. In other words, any who well know that Christ's sacrifice in their behalf is the only way to have access to God, and knowing that, turn their backs on Christ, are turning their backs on the desire for, or possibility of, communion with God. Such persons cannot even be brought to repentance (6:4).

The greater a person's belief in the danger of judgment and the magnitude of God's offer in Christ, the less likely that person is to yield to the temptation to sin. By the same token, such a person who does sin, does it in defiance of former faith, thereby making it less likely to find it possible to repent. The author of Hebrews has in mind, especially, Christians who have withdrawn from the church, some even to the point of disavowing Christ. Even to accept Christ as simply one of the many divinities in one of many cults was, for the Hebrews author, a deliberate sin. To be a Christian meant faith in the final and full revelation of God in Christ.

Some readers have interpreted the passage to mean that if one accepts Christ's sacrifice once and for all, then one is eternally secure. That is not the intent of the author of Hebrews because, in that case, there would be no need for this warning. Of course, the benefits of Christ's sacrifice endure, the author notes, for all time. But those who exclude themselves from fellowship with Christ thereby exclude themselves from those benefits.

The author could hardly present a more terrifying portent of judgment than *a fearful prospect* (verse 27). Like the return of Christ, so also the judgment is imminent. Hence, response to the writer's encouragement and warning should be right away. *Fire* was a frequent figure for disposal of the unrighteous, in Jewish thought. Rubbish was regularly disposed of in fires outside the gates of a city. So would the souls of those who reject salvation be disposed of, like rubbish.

A man who has violated the law alludes to capital punishment in the Mosaic law. It applied, for example, to blasphemy (Leviticus 24:16), murder (Numbers 35:30), idolatry (Deuteronomy 17:2-7; Numbers 25:5), and willful false prophecy (Deuteronomy 18:20). *How much worse* (a typical form of argument among the writer's contemporary rabbis; see 2:2-3) than all these crimes is that of spurning the Son of God.

Profaning *the blood of the covenant* is outraging the *Spirit of grace*. The great and mighty God graciously invites the undeserving sinner to come and, cleansed from sin, to approach God's presence. For the sinner to accept this honor and then turn and spurn God's gracious Spirit appalls the writer. *Spurned*, in Greek, is used for showing excessive contempt. Profaning the blood of the covenant means to disparage it, to despise Christ.

Verse 30 quotes two Old Testament texts, Deuteronomy 32:35 and 36 (Greek text). The writer interprets them, in support of his certainty of judgment, to say that God will punish all who rebel against divine mercy.

The living God, a phrase commonly used among the Jews, is a reminder of the power of an active God. Renegades will not get away with flouting him.

Recall Faith Experiences (10:32-34)

As before (6:2-3), the writer turns from sternly warning his readers to caring encouragement. This is an appeal to their memories, to the sincerity and eagerness of their early days as Christians. He praises them for their fortitude under outside pressure.

When were these *former days*? It is not clear, but the verb form suggests that it was just after their enlightenment. Their *enlightenment* (6:4) may allude to their baptism, or their being enlightened by the Holy Spirit. At that time they were subjected to struggle and suffering, yet they *endured* (verse 32). Sometimes they were publicly exposed, made a public spectacle, perhaps abused as a public entertainment. This and *affliction* (afflicted by persecutors) were increasingly the lot of early-day Christians. At other times, presumably when they could have avoided it, they were *partners*, they shared the sufferings of others who were being mistreated, bringing provisions to fellow Christians who were thrown into prison. It was common for persons accused of a crime to have their property plundered. Officials might confiscate it or allow it to be looted. Yet, the Christians knew they *had a better possession*, one that could not be touched: their salvation (see 13:14).

Persevere With Confidence (10:35-39)

These verses prepare the reader for the last lesson in the sermon, on faithful perseverance (Chapter 11).

Keep it up! says the writer. Hold on! Don't give up now. You endured. Endure a little longer. Christ will soon be here and you will have your promised reward. Do not throw away your confidence. After all the boldness and patience you have had as Christians, you will stand to lose it all if you do not continue firm in your faith. And you could lose it, you know, by *wavering* from your hope (verse 23), by neglecting your Christian fellowship (verse 25), by failing in your adherence to Christ. You have need of endurance. (The theme of patience will be enlarged on in 12:1-13.) You need to do the will of God (obedience like Christ's). Then you receive what is promised (as Abraham did; see 6:15).

In just *a little while . . . the coming one shall come*. This quotation from the Greek translation of Isaiah 26:20-21 and another free translation of Habakkuk 2:4 are used to buttress the readers' faith. The author has already stated that Christ will return (9:28). In verse 39, the author identifies with the Christians addressed in this sermon: *we are not of those who shrink back*. Those who shrink back lose their souls. *But the righteous shall live by his faith* (Habakkuk 2:4).

The author will now proceed (Chapter 11) to talk about those who have lived by faith.

§ § § § § § §

The Message of Hebrews 10:19-39

In this passage, the author mingles assurances about the effectiveness of Jesus as our high priest with encouragement to be faithful, to draw near to God, to stimulate each other in love and good deeds. The message is also a warning to those who might turn against Christ and deride what he has done for them.

The message warns us:

§ to recognize that God, who invites us to communion, is not a sentimental deity, but one who will not tolerate unrighteousness;

§ to understand that if we deliberately and willfully abandon our faith, if we disparage Christ and mock what he has done, if we flaunt God's gracious love for us, then we condemn ourselves to the worst possible punishment, the inability to come to God.

The message encourages us:

§ to think of a time in our lives when our Christian faith was most bouyant, when we best lived by it unflinchingly, when we witnessed it most clearly, when we endured suffering rather than compromise it;

§ to dare to care for those who are derided or persecuted on account of their Christian convictions;

§ to focus our attention on Christ and the meaning of his sacrifice for our sins;

§ to trust that we are forgiven and made clean;

§ to build each other up in faith and hope;

§ to do good things for others;

§ to be faithful in worshiping and meeting together;

§ to live expectantly, confident that the Day of the Lord is coming soon; and most of all

§ to persevere as we move toward God.

§ § § § § § §

PART ELEVEN Hebrews 11:1-22

Introduction to These Verses

The eleventh chapter of Hebrews is the fifth and final lesson of the sermon. It is about faith. It is about the goal toward which the life of faithfulness moves.

In this passage, the writer seeks to inspire the readers with great examples of persevering faith. To keep moving on in hope—that is the religion this sermon has proclaimed. Readers are urged to keep on in the same hope that inspired people of faith in times past. They lived by, and moved forward in, hope for what God has promised.

Here is an outline of Hebrews 11:1-22.
  I. Faith Is Confidence in the Expected (11:1-3)
  II. By Faith Abel and Enoch Pleased God (11:4-6)
  III. Noah: Heir of Righteousness (11:7)
  IV. Abraham Went Out in Faith (11:8-10)
  V. Sarah Trusted God's Promise (11:11-12)
  VI. Confidence in Things Hoped For (11:13-16)
  VII. Abraham and Isaac (11:17-19)
  VIII. Isaac, Jacob, and Joseph Trusted God (11:20-22)

Faith Is Confidence in the Expected (11:1-3)

These definitions of faith follow the quotation from the prophet Habakkuk (Habakkuk 2:4): *My righteous one shall live by faith* (10:38) and from the statement . . . *of those who have faith and keep their souls* (10:39).

The author needs to make sure the readers understand what is meant by faith. Chapters 5 through

10 contrast the old sanctuary, priesthood, sacrifices, and covenant with the new, heavenly sanctuary and the new covenant in Jesus Christ, who is the true high priest and the true sacrifice. The contrast is cast in terms of the shadow and the real. The old was merely shadows, reflections of the real which was yet to come. The old was inadequate, but at the same time it was a foreshadow of the perfect which was to come.

Now the writer goes on to show the faith of people who lived in the shadows, who experienced only the copies of the real. What made them of record was that they lived by trust in their hope of the real yet to come. For Hebrews, Christianity is a religion of hope. But it is a hope being realized by faith.

What is faith, then? Faith is based on the understanding that the world was created by the word of God. It is the word of God that is the permanently real. The world that this word created is secondary and not eternal. Faith cannot depend on the always changing world. It must look to the word behind the world. Faith must look from the copies, what is seen, to what they are made out of, the real, which do not appear. With this understanding, faith is the conviction of things not seen; the things being hoped for.

Assurance (verse 1) has been translated as *firm assurance, practical realization, steadfast expectation, visual anticipation, guarantee, certainty, essence,* even *possession.* All carry a sense of what the writer wishes to say.

Faith is the experience of hope. The same word, *faith,* is also used for faithfulness, and that connotation is also here—being faithful to what is believed in and expected. Such faith is demonstrated in the lives of those who live by faith in this hope. Their lives show faith in God, trust in *his saving power* (Psalm 78:22) in the future that has been promised. Hope that the promise will be fulfilled is what kept them faithful. It was this kind of faith which received divine approval.

By Faith Abel and Enoch Pleased God (11:4-6)

Abel and Enoch, two men from the ancient past, before the Flood, begin the record of faith and faithfulness in Hebrews. Both Abel and Enoch are illustrations of persons who pleased God by their faith.

Abel's story is found in Genesis 4:1-10. Abel was a shepherd and his brother Cain was *a tiller of the ground*. Cain made an offering to God of the *fruit of the ground*. Abel made an offering of the first lambs of the flock. Abel's offering was a more acceptable sacrifice to God than was Cain's. Genesis does not explain why, except that *sin is couching at the door* of Cain. Scholarly studies to explain the background of this ancient story would not concern the writer to the Hebrews. Hebrews simply accepts the story as told and explains only this important point: that Abel's offering was made *by faith*. Abel, for Hebrews, is an example of one who suffered for his faith and whose faith was such that he received approval as righteous. He does not compromise his righteousness, but dies for it. (This death of Abel is also spoken of in Matthew 23:35 and 1 John 3:12.) *But through his faith he is still speaking* is a reference to Genesis 4:10. Abel's shed blood cries out to God for justice. According to Hebrews, Abel, though murdered, continues as a witness to faith.

The story of Enoch walking with God is told briefly in Genesis 5:24. The Greek translation read by the author of Hebrews includes the words *he pleased God*. Hebrews quotes this and says that *by faith* he was *taken up*, removed or withdrawn from the visible world. The implication, which Hebrews affirms, is that Enoch did not see death. Before he was taken up, however, Enoch *walked with God* (Genesis 5:22). Faith is a desire to be with God, to have fellowship with God. Basic to such faith is a firm belief that God exists and rewards those who respond in faith. The reward is the fellowship with God they hope for and seek. Such faith is a movement by the believer to draw near, approach, come toward God.

Here is the fourth "impossible" in Hebrews. All have to do with faith and the goal of fellowship with God. (1) Without faith in God, there can be no pleasing God, and so no fellowship with God (11:6). (2) Fellowship cannot be attained by those who reject faith (6:4). (3) Sin, the barrier to faith and fellowship, is not removable by formal, external religion (10:4). (4) Yet, God's purpose and offer of fellowship are always available to the faithful (6:18).

Noah: Heir of Righteousness (11:7)

Noah demonstrated his confidence in God's intentions by building the ark when, as yet, there was no evidence of the flood. Noah's story appears in Genesis 6:5–9:17.

Noah's faith is shown in four ways in this verse. First, he was devout. The word for holy awe of God is almost lost in the translation *took heed*. It could be said that Noah's attitude of faith was the reason God spoke to him. Second, he responded to events *as yet unseen*, thus characterizing the definition of faith in verse 1: *the conviction of things not seen*. Third, he responded to the message of warning. The author wants the readers to show faith by heeding the warnings given. Fourth, he responded with action.

There were two consequences of Noah's faith action. First, by it he condemned the world. His building the ark, although it may have brought on ridicule by others, showed them up for their lack of faith. Because they had no faith, they were not ready for the deluge when it came. There was a tradition, apparently, that Noah had preached to the people, but they paid no attention. Noah is called *a herald of righteousness* (2 Peter 2:5).

Second, he became an *heir of the righteouness which comes by faith*, distinct from the superficial righteousness which comes by observance of law. Noah's righteousness was inherent in his faith. Like Enoch, the person of faith (Noah) moves by faith toward God, the reward of his faith.

Abraham Went Out in Faith (11:8-10)

The story about Abraham begins in Genesis 12:1. It parallels the story of Noah. Noah built an ark at God's bidding without any visible evidence of its need at first. Abraham left his hometown at God's bidding without any evidence of the Promised Land which he was to receive as an inheritance.

Abraham's faith shows in three ways. First, he obeyed God's call. The verb form used by Hebrews indicates no hesitation. Called, he went. Another first-century writer, Philo, dramatized the incident, telling about the trauma Abraham and his family went through in cutting off all ties with their home and past. Hebrews notes only Abraham's forward-looking faith action. He moved out at God's call, toward the unseen, not knowing where he was to go (Genesis 12:1-2).

Second, he lived as an alien in a foreign land. He lived in tents, which were temporary dwellings, because he was only a sojourner. Isaac and Jacob, his son and grandson, also recipients of the promise, lived with him in tents. Abraham had moved out from the past. He did not put down roots in the present. He looked forward to a future devised by God. Hebrews (in 3:11-12 and 4:11) has already warned Christians from stopping short of the goal toward which they are headed. People of faith do not settle down in this world. Its culture is not theirs. They are sojourners on their way.

Looking ahead is the third element of Abraham's faith. *He looked forward to the city which has foundations, whose builder and maker is God.* This statement fits the pattern of "shadow and reality" in the writer's teaching, like the contrasts between the earthly institutions of religion and the heavenly reality. Abraham looked for a heavenly city, made by God, not by human devisement and artifice. This is like *the true tent which is set up not by man but by the Lord* (8:2). This real city to which God calls the faithful will be cited again in 11:16; 12:22; 13:14.

Sarah Trusted God's Promise (11:11-12)

Sarah was a partner with Abraham in his faith in God's promise of heirs. They were both old, and she had borne no child. The story is found in Genesis 17:15-16; 18:1-15; 21:1-7. Sarah laughed when told that she was to bear a child at her advanced age. But the Lord said, *Is anything too hard for the* LORD? (Genesis 18:14). The Greek text suggests that this was a fourth element in Abraham's faith, that he received strength to father a child. Hebrews, however, makes Sarah herself the subject. It was by her faith, with that of her husband, that she received the power to conceive. It was Sarah's venture of faith. She considered him faithful who had promised. (See Romans 4:18-21 for Paul's similar account.) God would not fail in fulfilling the promise. *He who promised is faithful* (10:23). Here was a faith action. The Greek of verse 12 expresses how remarkable this was: *Wherefore, indeed!* from a man whose body had died, so far as its use in propagation was concerned, nevertheless was to have descendants, as many as the stars of heaven and as the innumerable grains of sand by the seashore (Genesis 15:5-6; 22:17).

Confidence in Things Hoped For (11:13-16)

These forebears of Israel never saw the fulfillment of God's promise, but they lived by the certainty that it would be. They were alien residents in Canaan. They were not homesick for the land from which they had come. They were seeking a homeland. They were not reticent about it. They made it clear. Others might not see it; they had seen it. This is one of the qualities of faith in Hebrews. The faithful see the seen as copies of the unseen truth. The seen directs their attention to the unseen of which the seen are copies. Those without faith do not see beyond the formal, earthly copies and so do not move forward in their lives toward the goal of the real. Having seen *what was promised . . .* they *greeted it from afar.*

Here is another of the "ifs" typical in Hebrews: *If they had been thinking of that land from which they had gone out, they would have had opportunity to return.* They were examples for the Christians who, according to Hebrews, do not belong to the past, nor tie themselves to the present. They were strangers and exiles on the earth (see Genesis 23:4; Leviticus 25:23). They belong to God's future. They move from the shadow toward the real. The real is a better country, that is, a heavenly one. The Old Testament reminds the reader that we are sojourners because our lifetime is limited. For Hebrews, this is a recognition that nothing earthly is ours or worth our attachment (1 Chronicles 29:15; Psalm 39:12).

God is called the God of Abraham, Isaac, and Jacob because they were men of faith. Of such people God is not ashamed to be called their God, for God has prepared for them a city (see John 14:2).

Abraham and Isaac (11:17-19)

A fifth element of Abraham's faith is his obedience to God. God tested his faith. The story is taken from Genesis 22:1-19. *God said to Abraham, "Take your son, your only son, Isaac, whom you love . . . and offer him . . . as a burnt offering . . ."* Sacrifice of first-born children was not uncommon in the ancient Middle East. However, Isaac was the son born to Abraham's old age, whom God had promised would be the ancestor of Abraham's posterity. It was a severe test of Abraham's faith. Would he be obedient to the terrible command? He could tell himself that God's command could not be genuine, since it ran counter to the promise. He could withhold that which was dear to him. But Abraham was obedient, trusting that God's promise would not fail. He considered that God was able to raise persons even from the dead. Somehow, although beyond human understanding, God the Creator could do the impossible (see Matthew 3:9). Figuratively speaking, God did snatch Isaac from death. God said, *Do not lay your hand on the lad or do anything to him; for now I know that you fear God, seeing you have not withheld your son, your only son, from me . . . I will indeed bless you . . . because you have obeyed my voice* (Genesis 22:12, 16-17).

Isaac, Jacob, and Joseph Trusted God (11:20-22)

The blessings which the patriarchs of Israel spoke were made in their confidence that God's promises would come true. A blessing was a pronouncement that had something of the sacred about it. It was a wish and will pronounced over the future of the individual receiving it. Pronounced by a righteous person near death, it carried a certainty about its being fulfilled. It was not a fortune-telling because it had to be realistic, made in terms either of the blesser's spiritual power or of the possessions and potential of blesser and the blessed. However, according to Hebrews these blessings, given by Israel's forebears, were based not on earthly possessions but on God's promises.

Isaac's blessing on Jacob and Esau is found in Genesis 27. The blessing, even though won by Jacob through guile, could not be taken away once pronounced. *Yes, and he shall be blessed* (Genesis 27:33). It was according to God's will that he should receive the promise.

The story of Jacob's blessing on his grandsons, Ephraim and Manasseh, and through his son, Joseph, is from Genesis 48:14-16 where Jacob's new God-given name (Israel) is used. Jacob, in the Genesis story, expresses his trust in God *who has led me all my life long to this day*. This God of promise will multiply the descendants of Jacob's grandchildren. *Bowing in worship over the head of his staff* is from the author's Greek translation of Genesis 47:31.

Joseph, at the end of his life (see Genesis 50:24-25) gave directions concerning his burial, that *you shall carry up my bones from here*. He was certain that the Israelites, although now in Egypt, would eventually be making their way to the land of God's promise.

§ § § § § § §

The Message of Hebrews 11:1-22

This passage defines faith in the God who created the universe. The hope of faith is the assurance of what God has planned and promised. The expression of faith is movement toward the fulfillment that God has promised. Faith is faithfulness to God and to Christ who opens the way to God. Ultimately, faith is the foretaste of the experience of living in God's presence eternally.

The message of this passage is encouragement seen in the faith of persons who trusted in God's promises.

Through these examples, Hebrews says to Christians:

§ You cannot depend on the material world; it is imperfect, never permanent, and uncertain.

§ You can depend on the existence of God whose word created the world.

§ Learn faith from the lives of people who have lived by faith.

§ Live to please God and you will know God's approval.

§ You can depend on the purpose of God which includes you.

§ God calls you to leave your attachment to the past, move out to God's presence, and do what is God's righteous will for you.

§ Realize that the impossible is possible if God calls you to do it.

§ Recognize that, as a Christian, you are an alien, a sojourner in this world. Its standards and culture and practices are not yours.

§ Be obedient to God. Hold nothing back, as though it were more precious to you than God.

§ Make your plans in the light of God's purpose.

§ § § § § § §

PART TWELVE Hebrews 11:23-40

Introduction to These Verses

This passage, gathering momentum as it goes, continues the record of heroes of faith. It covers nearly a thousand years of Jewish history with accounts of courage and commitment. The author's words paint a picture of faith that endures, of people—individuals and an entire nation—whose confidence in God and in where God was leading them made them spurn both the wealth and pleasures offered and the persecution threatened by the world.

Besides persons named in the passage, others, unnamed, are suggestive of Old Testament heroes.

Six characteristics of faith strongly mark this series: action, courage, unhesitating choice, identity with the people of God, obedience, and readiness to suffer, endure, and persevere rather than recede from the goal of faith.

Here is an outline of Hebrews 11:23-40.
I. Moses Lived by Faith (11:23-28)
II. Israel Came to Canaan by Faith (11:29-31)
III. Strong Leaders and Prophets (11:32-34)
IV. Faith in Times of Suffering (11:35-38)
V. Faith in God's Promise (11:39-40)

Moses Lived by Faith (11:23-28)

These verses are about the faith of Moses, from his infancy to his leadership in Israel.

The first expression of his faith is really that of his

parents, or of his mother (see Exodus 1:22–2:3). The king had ordered that all male children born to Hebrew mothers should be killed. Moses' parents were not afraid of the king's edict because their faith found a way to save the baby, who was beautiful.

The story of the discovery of the baby, Moses, and of the child's adoption by the king's daughter, is told in Exodus 2:4-10. Brought up as a royal son, Moses could have lived in the wealth and pleasures of the pharaoh's family, if he had renounced his Hebrew connection. Instead, he chose to be ill-treated along with the people of God. This was the second expression of his faith. It is the writer's hint to the Christians not to give up their faith, even though it involved suffering.

For Hebrews, Christ, through whom God *created the world* (1:2), is present in all the words of God and actions of God in the Bible. Hence, he could say that Moses *considered abuse suffered for Christ greater wealth than the treasures of Egypt*. The main concern in mentioning Christ here is to encourage Christians to prefer persecution for Christ's sake than life apart from Christian faith. All they needed to do to escape any unpleasantness on account of their Christian faith was to renounce their allegiance to Christ. *For he looked to the reward* is the fulfillment of God's promise, which, translated for the Christian readers, meant fellowship with God.

By faith he left Egypt. This, the third expression of his faith, probably refers to the story in Exodus 2:11-15. When Pharaoh heard of it, he sought to kill Moses. Moses was not *afraid of the anger of the king*. His faith, Hebrews is saying, drew Moses to a better way. Hebrews presents Moses as an example of the patience urged on the readers. Moses endured because he had the faith that sees him who is invisible, *the conviction of things not seen* (11:1). The Exodus passage says that Moses was afraid. For this reason, some commentators think that the reference in Hebrews is not to Moses' personal flight to

Midian, but to his boldness in leading Israel out of Egypt.

The fourth expression of Moses' faith is his celebration of the first Passover. This story is told in Exodus 12:1-24. The night the Lord destroyed the first-born of Egypt (Exodus 11:4-6), he passed over the Israelites who, following Moses' example, sprinkled the blood of the Passover lamb *on the two doorposts and the lintel* (Exodus 12:7, 23). This, too, showed that Moses' and the Israelites' trust in God was greater than any fear of the anger of the king.

Israel Came to Canaan by Faith (11:29-31)

The incidents in Israel's exodus from Egypt are marked as acts of faith. As usual in Hebrews, faith is associated with action, and action, as usual, is movement toward a divinely promised goal.

The first incident Hebrews takes from the migration account is based on Exodus 14. Israel was up against seemingly impossible odds, a slave people fleeing from the power of Egypt. As Hebrews presents it, however, this was an action of faith, not of fear. They were not fleeing from Egyptian power as much as they were going out into the desert, into the unknown, toward the land God had promised, for they had faith in that promise. So they *crossed the Red Sea as if on dry land*. The Egyptians were not activated by faith. They were drowned, or as the Greek picturesquely put it, they were swallowed up by the sea.

The second incident is of Israel's first success in Canaan. The story is found in Joshua 6. The fall of Jericho was not by force of arms. For seven days the Israelite army marched around Jericho following the ark of the covenant, which represented the presence of God. On the seventh day they marched around Jericho seven times. The priests blew their ram's horns and the walls of Jericho fell down. They did not trust in their own strength; God had promised them the land of Canaan, and they placed their confidence in that promise.

These two great events came about *by faith,* according to the writer of Hebrews.

Associated with the story of the taking of Jericho is the story of Rahab, the prostitute. This story is the subject of Joshua 2. Israelite spies had come to Jericho. They stayed in Rahab's house. A prostitute's home would be a likely place for strange men to remain in the city without detection. Their presence was discovered, however. The king of Jericho demanded that Rahab deliver them. Instead, she hid them, misdirected their pursuers, and saved them by advising them how to escape. She did this because, as she said, *I know that the* LORD *has given you the land . . . for the* LORD *your God is he who is God in heaven above and on earth beneath* (Joshua 2:9, 11).

The point of Hebrews 11:31 is that it was because of this faith in God and the promise to Israel that Rahab saved the spies. Besides saving them, her faith was the reason she (with her family, see Joshua 2:12-14) was saved when Israel subdued the city of Jericho. Rahab had seen beyond the immediate situation to the greater things that God had promised.

Strong Leaders and Prophets (11:32-34)

All the truly great leaders and genuine prophets throughout Israel's history, says the writer of Hebrews, accomplished great things because of their faith in God's promise.

The list is a long one, so the writer does not detail their stories. These stories are found in Judges 6–8 (Gideon); Judges 4–5 (Barak); Judges 13–16 (Samson); Judges 11–12 (Jephthah). The stories of Samuel are found mostly in First Samuel. The stories about David are found in First and Second Samuel, First Chronicles, and Chapters 1 and 2 of First Kings. The prophets are not named. The brief listing suggests that Hebrews especially had in mind Elijah (1 Kings 19) and Elisha (2 Kings 6).

What did they do *through faith*? They *conquered kingdoms* and *enforced justice*. They *received promises*. This could be said of all the persons named. Obtaining promises could also mean that they saw all the promises fulfilled. The same verb is used of Abraham in Hebrews 6:15: *Abraham obtained the promise*. Here the promises are plural. The writer of Hebrews probably had in mind the statement in Joshua 21:44-45: *And the LORD gave them rest on every side just as he had sworn to their fathers . . . Not one of all the good promises which the LORD had made to the house of Israel had failed*. These leaders and prophets all received promises of God's help which they realized as they acted out their faith.

Stopped the mouths of lions is reminiscent of Daniel in the lions' den (Daniel 6:16-22; see also 1 Samuel 17:34-37; 2 Samuel 23:20). *Quenched raging fire* suggests Daniel's three friends in the fiery furnace (Daniel 3:19-20).

The sharp edges of the sword were, figuratively, called "mouths." This is the word used by Hebrews in the Greek text. *Mouths* of the sword corresponds to *mouths* of lions (verse 33). The sword was often spoken of in Jewish writings as devouring those it killed. The phrase here, *escaped the edge of the sword*, is a figure of speech and means, in more general terms, escaped murder or assassination. There were many such escapes recorded in stories of Elijah (1 Kings 19:1-14) and Elisha (2 Kings 6:30-32).

The Greek words in verse 33, *won strength out of weakness*, suggest power given individuals who are weak, such as David meeting Goliath (1 Samuel 17). This striking juxtaposition of the words for *power* and *weakness* makes vivid the effectiveness of faith in the lives of the faithful, such as was expressed in the Lord's answer to the prayer of Paul, the apostle: *My power is made perfect in weakness* (2 Corinthians 12:9). Stories that dramatize God's power in human weakness are frequent in the Old Testament, as in 1 Kings 19 and 2 Kings 6:15-17. This phrase has also been translated as *recovered from illness*, as with King Hezekiah of Judah who, after praying to God, was restored to health because of his life of faithfulness (Isaiah 38:1-5).

David, starting out as a shepherd boy, came to be celebrated for his military triumphs (see 1 Samuel 18:7). The phrase *became mighty in war* (verse 34) could also be ascribed to many judges and kings in Israel's history. This phrase and the remaining phrase, *put foreign armies to flight*, more likely refer to the battles of the Israelites for independence from the Greek-Syrian empire in the second century before Christ.

Faith in Times of Suffering (11:35-38)

These verses review the courageous faith of Jews, especially during the times of persecution in the second century B.C. when the Greek-Syrian Emperor, Antiochus, tried to enforce pagan worship and practice on them. This was the century when belief in resurrection became current among Jews. Since they did not see righteousness fulfilled in the world of their experience, many concluded that they were seeing only a part of the process. They thought there must be a future in God's plan that would be perfected in a heavenly place where righteousness and truth would prevail.

Women received their dead by resurrection. There are two stories associated with the prophets Elijah (1 Kings 17:17-24) and Elisha (2 Kings 4:32-37) about the restoration of life to children who had died. Each was the son of a woman of extraordinary faith, and the prophets were able to restore them to life.

The rest of the examples of suffering and endurance probably come from accounts of Greek-Syrian oppression and the Jewish revolt which began in 167 B.C. *Some were tortured, refusing to accept release*: One of the famous stories :riod, narrated in the book of Second Maccabees, a certain Eleazar who could have avoided torture and death if he had eaten pork as commanded to do by his torturers. Eating pork is against Jewish law (Leviticus 11:7-8), and to do so was considered a despicable renunciation of Jewish faith (Isaiah 65:4). He was beaten with an iron bar which broke the bones of the body and finally crushed the chest. The Greek word for *torture* is literally *drummed upon*. This meaning may also refer to the block on which the victim was stretched for the beating. Such a death was preferred by the faithful to violation of their faith. Its consequence was resurrection to *a better life*. The author adds this as a counsel to persecuted Christians: Endure, as pioneers in the faith did, because if you persevere, you will come to *a better life* than the life you would have if you saved yourself by turning from Christ.

Some faced *mocking and scourging*, while still others were chained and put in prison.

Stories of victories against great odds, and the stories of incidents and sufferings listed in verses 33-39, were recited among the Jews in the time of the writing of Hebrews. Many are still recalled in the Jewish celebration of Hanukkah each year. They celebrate the period shortly before and during the time of the Jewish wars for independence. Many of these stories are found in the writings known as *Apocrypha*. The sufferings could also apply to courageous prophets of an earlier period. The sufferings of the prophet Jeremiah were well known (Jeremiah 20:1-2; 37:15; 38:6), as were the sufferings of the prophets Micaiah (1 Kings 22:24-27) and Hanani (2 Chronicles 16:7-10).

They were stoned, as was the prophet Zechariah (2 Chronicles 24:20-22). There was also a tradition that Jeremiah was killed by stoning in Egypt. *They were sawn in two*: Isaiah was sawn in two with a wooden sword, according to tradition. *They were killed with the sword* echoes a statement in 1 Kings 19:10: *The people . . . have slain thy prophets with the sword*. The prophet Uriah was killed by the sword (Jeremiah 26:23). *Of whom the world was not worthy* is a phrase used by early Jewish writers about persons or commands of God far superior to the world which cast them out as unworthy.

Faith in God's Promise (11:39-40)

The faith catalogue in Chapter 11 is summed up with five implicit declarations about the heroes mentioned:

(1) They all acted in firm confidence in God's promise. Their faith-heroism is *well attested*, certified.

(2) However, they did not receive what was promised. They were still, in the imagery of Hebrews, under the old covenant in the earthly sanctuary. The way into the heavenly sanctuary was not *opened as long as the outer tent is still standing* (9:8).

(3) The fulfillment of the promise was reserved for our time. God had foreseen our time as the right time for the Day of the Lord. The *better* was the coming of Christ as God's fullest revelation (1:1), the ultimate sacrifice, to perfect us, to purify us (9:14).

(4) Our fulfillment is possible with our consecration in God's presence. To *be made perfect* is to be made complete, to have fully arrived. The heroes of faith could not be complete without us, for God's plans included us. They could not fully arrive until this age should be consummated in Christ's coming.

(5) Those heroes of the past can join with us in God's presence. Christ will return and gather us all together (9:28).

§ § § § § § §

The Message of Hebrews 11:23-40

This section of the faith chapter in Hebrews gives more examples of heroic persons who persevered by faith in God's promise. Great examples for us of faith in action are: Moses, the people of Israel, Rahab, leaders and prophets of Israel, and innumerable men and women who endured suffering rather than giving up or compromising their faith in God's promise for something better and greater ahead. None received the promise in their times. Nevertheless, they had such firm confidence in it that they lived by hope. Now, as God has planned, they, with us, receive the fulfillment of God's promise.

These examples were given as a message for Christians, that we should:

§ live by faith;

§ grow in faith in a world which will give us no support in our obedience to God;

§ live not for material things but for spiritual goals;

§ be faithful to Christ, knowing that being Christ's person is worth more than all the treasure in the world;

§ never compromise with the world; prefer suffering, homelessness, prison, persecution, death, to losing Christ;

§ fearlessly ignore demands of the world which run counter to our faith in God;

§ wholly identify with God's people, even if it means leaving the old crowd or being derided by them;

§ move fearlessly in the direction of the hope to which God calls us;

§ patiently persevere with confidence in God's purpose, trusting in God's power to do great and mighty things;

§ face seemingly impossible obstacles without fear, knowing that God can strengthen us through faith.

§ § § § § § §

PART THIRTEEN: Hebrews 12:1-17

Introduction to These Verses

The sermon comes to a close with a fifth and final section of counsel (12:1–13:17). Throughout the eleventh chapter the main intent of the author of Hebrews has been to encourage Christians in their faith by recording the power of faith and faithfulness in the lives of heroes of the past. This encouragement is now focused on the foremost of all faithful ones, Jesus Christ. Looking to him, counsels the writer, you can persevere through hardship toward your God-given goals.

Aware of whatever sufferings the Christians have been through, the author reminds them that they are still alive. They should accept suffering as a discipline God sends them to strengthen them. Then they can do their best, and live in peace and thankfulness.

Here is an outline of Hebrews 12:1-17.
I. Follow Jesus in Faith (12:1-2)
II. Persevere Through Suffering (12:3-6)
III. Discipline Leads to Righteousness (12:7-11)
IV. Therefore, Be Strong (12:12-13)
V. Live in Peace and Goodness (12:14-17)

Follow Jesus in Faith (12:1-2)

For Hebrews, the Christian life is one of movement toward a goal. The writer uses a metaphor, frequent in old Greek writings, of life as a strenuous race. The race course is before us. All around us, as witnesses, are the crowd of heroes who have already run well the race of faith. We, the author included, are the runners, stripped (of sin) for the race. We are determined and we must persevere in the race of faith (the same metaphor is used in Philippians 3:13-14). The race requires endurance, essential in the practice of faith.

The greatest of all expressions of faith is seen in Jesus. He has already run the course. He ran it with perseverence, enduring the cross. He ran with joy. He attained the prize: the seat at the right hand of God (Psalm 110:1). We are to keep our eyes on him, enduring as he did. For us, too, there is the prize, the presence of God.

The heroes of the faith are spoken of as a great *cloud of witnesses*. Their lives are a witness to us. Their lives have shown us how to run, how to endure. They, also, are witnesses watching how we run our course. We are watched from above.

Besides the need for endurance is the necessity of laying aside, throwing off, anything that encumbers or hinders us. Like a runner who must put aside any weight, we are to leave off anything, no matter how good or harmless it may seem in itself, that will in any way hamper us or impede the serious business of the Christian life. We must be free to move toward God.

Sin is difficult to get rid of because it *clings so closely*. The unusual adjective Hebrews uses to describe sin has been translated in several different ways, but generally it means sins which we find it hard to part with. In other contexts in Greek literature, the word has been used to mean *easily avoided*, *dangerous*, even *admired*. A very early manuscript of Hebrews uses another word, different by one stroke of the pen in Greek, which means *easily distracting* sin. It must be cast off because it entangles us, trips us up.

The word *race* means *contest, toil, peril*. The English word *agony* comes from the same Greek root. Running a good race is not finding out what one is comfortable with. Running calls for *perseverance*, Hebrews' emphasis on endurance.

Jesus is the supreme example to inspire us. Our attention must be fixed on him (*look to Jesus*, verse 2), on no one and on nothing else. He is *the pioneer . . . of our faith*, indeed, the author of our faith. In his earthly course he showed us how to run. He leads the way. He is the *perfecter of our faith* in that he embodies and completes it. Jesus *endured the cross*. This is the only time Hebrews specifies the cross. There are clear references to the crucifixion, however (5:8; 6:6; 9:25-28; 13:12), and many references to Jesus' suffering.

The readers had suffered only a little. Greater suffering than any other shall have was Jesus' suffering on the cross, a tortured death as a criminal exposed to public derision. Nevertheless, *despising the shame*, Jesus accepted the shame and torture as a small matter in the light of his goal. That goal could be reached only by way of the cross (5:8). The goal, to cleanse people of sin (9:26) and to open up a way for people to God (10:20-21) was worth the suffering. The goal recalls the declaration of Paul: *For his sake I have suffered the loss of all things, and count them as refuse, in order that I may gain Christ* (Philippians 3:8). *The joy* sustained him even through suffering itself because it was a suffering self-sacrifice endured *for everyone* (2:9-10). *Set before him* is the same verb as in *the race that is set before us* (verse 1) and in *the hope that is set before us* (6:18). His goal is ours.

Persevere Through Suffering (12:3-6)

The writer returns to the second person. The Christians addressed had evidently been surprised and troubled by their suffering. Perhaps they had not expected that the Christian faith involved suffering, and they were faltering in their Christian loyalty because of it. The writer reminds them that Jesus, who was the source of their faith, had suffered more than any of them. They had not suffered to the shedding of their blood. Look at it this way, says the writer: Suffering, no matter who brings it upon you, can be for you a discipline by which God would help you.

The quotation is from Proverbs 3:11-12. This proverb counsels: (1) Do not struggle through hard times without learning from them or growing in faith. That would be to *regard lightly the discipline of the Lord*. (2) Do not *lose courage*. Do not give in by giving up in whimpering complaint against God.

What Christians are asked to endure is nothing in comparison with what Christ *endured from sinners*—for them. *Hostility against himself* was literally *contradictions*: the controversies that filled Jesus' ministry as many in Judea attempted to oppose and undo his work and message. If the readers consider Jesus, keep their attention on him, they *may not grow weary or faint-hearted*. The same verb is used in a similar counsel in Galatians 6:9: *And let us not grow weary in well-doing, for in due season we shall reap, if we do not lose heart.*

You have not yet resisted suggests that they had not gone as far as Christians may at times need to go. Bold witness of their faith might arouse persecution as it did for some of the heroes of faith recounted in Chapter 11. The people addressed in this sermon had not faced martyrdom, *shedding your blood*.

The word in Greek, *discipline*, comes from the word for *child* and relates to upbringing, training, instructing, and educating a child. This involves discipline and correction as a part of the child's guidance. The word is appropriate for a father's love for his child. He *chastises*. The word is used for flogging or other stiff punishment thought to be necessary for the child's development. Hebrews says that through the experience of suffering for their faith, Christians can know that they are accepted by God as God's children. The Lord receives as his child (*whom he receives*) any who come to learn from him.

Discipline Leads to Righteousness (12:7-11)

The writer discusses the value of discipline for the Christian. All people undergo discipline of one sort or another. The discipline God gives leads to holy sharing with God. It is a training for peace and right.

It is for discipline that you have to endure (verse 7). Whatever you have to go through, take it as part of your training for Christian living. *God is treating you as sons.* By disciplining us, God behaves toward us as a father behaves with his children. To think that God would protect good people from pain is to misconceive God and goodness. We respect parents who discipline us. Parents who take no interest in their children's training deserve no respect. Their children are no better off than homeless orphans. We, if we do not *subject*, that is, submit, ourselves to God's discipline, cannot consider ourselves God's children. We are, then, no better than illegitimates, *without discipline.* Who said that being a Christian is easy! (See Matthew 7:13-14.) Escaping God's discipline cuts us off from being one with suffering of all Christians.

Father of spirits is an unusual phrase. The writer was familiar with the Book of Numbers where Moses appeals to God as *God of the spirits of all flesh* (Numbers 16:22; 27:16). Our parents disciplined us as it seemed good to them. God disciplines us for our benefit. And what is that benefit? That, by submitting to God, we shall truly live (verse 9). Also, it means that *we may share his holiness.* We participate in God's holiness as we come into God's holy presence.

All discipline *seems painful rather than pleasant.* The King James Version accurately translates that discipline seems *not joyous but grievous.* It is difficult for the Christian to sense joy in the midst of grief and pain. The result of endurance is joy, however. John's Gospel illustrates the same idea: A woman's anguish in childbirth is replaced by joy in the child that is born (John 16:21). The illustration in Hebrews is that of an athlete. The training is rigorous, but the result of the training is—and here the metaphor changes—*the peaceful fruit of righteousness*. This is what the rest of the sermon and closing letter is about: the well-being of a life that is in line with God's righteous goodness. This peace, longed for in the struggle of pain, is also the peace that comes with the self-control that discipline teaches. A person is no longer self-assertive and quarrelsome when obedient under God's discipline.

Therefore, Be Strong (12:12-13)

The Christians to whom the sermon is addressed apparently complain because the way has been hard, their strength limited. Since the purpose of God's discipline is to strengthen us, we must contribute our own effort to be strong. An indolent and self-pitying child does not profit from training. Patients who do not exercise their limbs do not benefit from medical therapy. An athlete who makes no strenuous effort will not reach the goal.

Continuing the analogy of physical achievement, the writer is using phrases borrowed from the Greek Old Testament (Isaiah 35:3 and Proverbs 4:26). Hands that have grown weary and knees that have become paralyzed were used as metaphors for persons who had given up, despaired, or even turned cowardly. The phrase *weak-kneed* is still used in the same way.

The racecourse metaphor applies to *straight paths*. The Greek word *paths* is used here for rutted tracks made by the wheels of a vehicle. This could make for difficult running. The *lame* (dislocated) leg could *be put out of joint*. Therefore, the runner needs to smooth out the running path, that the leg may have a chance to *be healed*.

Live in Peace and Goodness (12:14-17)

Christians can be on their way to God, to *see the Lord*, if they maintain personal purity, good relationships, and identity among themselves.

Christians are to make every effort to live in peace with all fellow-Christians (see Psalm 34:14). *Strive for peace* can be translated as *follow peace*. The writer continues to stress that the way of faith is in action, movement, and effort. There are hints that relations among the Christians may not have been altogether harmonious (3:12-13; 4:11; 10:24-25; 13:1, 16-17). *And for the holiness* means that Christians are to belong to the fellowship of the saints, people made holy by God's presence. The goal of the Christian life, to see the Lord, is shared holiness (verse 10).

By our failures in Christian living it is possible that fellow Christians may become deficient in or even lose the experience of God's grace (*that no one fail to obtain the grace of God*, verse 15). The writer has in mind a passage in Deuteronomy 29:18: *Beware lest there be among you any whose heart turns away this day from the* LORD *. . . lest there be among you a root bearing poisonous and bitter fruit*. Such a root can *cause trouble, and by it the many become defiled* [tainted, corrupted].

Examples of corrupting influences would be an *immoral or irreligious* person. The word for *immoral* here is used for a fornicator. The word here translated *irreligious* is used as the contrary to the word *holiness* (verse 14). It refers to one whose life is worldly, separate from the holy group of pilgrims on their way to God. Esau was characterized by the rabbis as a fornicator. He lost the inheritance, which, in the language of the writer of Hebrews, was tantamount to losing the pathway that leads to God's promise. Esau's problem, of which Christians need to be wary, was that he put greater value on the momentary, worldly pleasure than on the inheritance God had for him. He *sold his birthright* [to his father's inheritance] *for a single meal*. The story is found in Genesis 25:29-30. The example is a warning to Christians not to surrender, in the stress of their temporary suffering, their inheritance in Christ.

The younger brother, Jacob, tricked their father, Isaac, into giving him the blessing due to the eldest son. A blessing thus given was thought of as a promise of future fulfillment and it was irrevocable once given. When Esau came to his father, it was in vain that he sought the blessing. It was too late. Hebrews' warning is clear—God has made an irrevocable promise which will be fulfilled. If, like Esau, Christians give up their birthright as *sons* (verses 7-8), rejecting God's promise, they lose their inheritance forever. *He was rejected* by Isaac because the blessing was irrevocable. Esau exemplifies the kind of person who excludes himself (as in 6:4-6). The dramatic story of Esau's tears and inability to regain the blessing he lost is found in Genesis 27:30-38. The writer does not say that Esau repented but that he *found no chance to repent*. He wanted the blessing, but he found no place for repentance. The warning, frequent in Hebrews, is not that God refuses the repentant ones, but that they go so far against Christ that they lose the capacity to repent. Some translators and commentators consider that it was Isaac who *found no chance to repent*, that is, that he saw no way he could change the situation.

§ § § § § § §

The Message of Hebrews 12:1-17

The writer asks Christians:
§ to let past heroes of faith spur us to a life of vigorous faith;
§ to resolutely follow the course God sets before us;
§ to cast aside anything that hampers total dedication;
§ to keep our eyes always on Jesus, who has opened for us the way to God;
§ to let Christ's example keep us from giving up;
§ to accept hardships as disciplines from God to teach us courage;
§ to take every difficulty as a discipline from God who loves us;
§ to persevere through hardship as a means of subjecting ourselves to God who makes us alive;
§ to keep remembering that if we endure through painful experiences, we will come to experience peace and goodness;
§ to make every effort to increase our spiritual strength, knowing our weaknesses and working on them;
§ to take responsibility to improve our lives in God's will;
§ to act in goodwill and dedication with fellow Christians, running the course of faith with them;
§ to avoid attitudes that will cause trouble for others;
§ to beware lest we put off and lose altogether the heritage God planned for us.

§ § § § § § §

PART FOURTEEN Hebrews 12:18-29

Introduction to These Verses

The new covenant is the joyful fulfillment God offers you. Through references to the Old Testament Scriptures, the Hebrews sermon reminds Christians of the joy that comes with obedience to God. It also warns them of the awful consequences of neglecting God's goodness to them. The sermon closes with a call to worship and gratitude.

Here is an outline of Hebrews 12:18-29.
I. Yours Is Not a Religion of Fear (12:18-21)
II. Come to the Joyful City of God (12:22-24)
III. Do Not Refuse God Who Calls You (12:25-27)
IV. Worship God With Thankfulness (12:28-29)

Yours Is Not a Religion of Fear (12:18-21)

This highly dramatic, colorful passage builds on the warning implicit in the previous passage against failing to obtain God's grace (verses 15-17). It also returns to the contrast between the old covenant and the new. It is an allegory of two mountains, representing the old and new covenants. The unbearable awesomeness of Mount Sinai, where the old covenant was given, is the converse to the peace and serenity of the heavenly Mount Zion where the new covenant is instituted. The vocabulary in these verses on the old covenant paints a sound-filled picture of a volcanic eruption.

The opening phrase begins the antithesis to the positive statement in verses 22-24: *Not come...*(verse 18) contrasts with *But you have come...*(verse 22). *To what may be touched* begins a sonorous series of works: *a blazing fire,* not an ordinary hearth fire but a raging fire, not a fire of light but of *darkness, and gloom, and a tempest*: a whirlwind of smoke. *The sound of a trumpet* is the sound of a war trumpet with its deafening blast.

The scene culminates with the thunderous voice of God (Deuteronomy 4:11-13) pronouncing the covenant. The terrifying picture from which Hebrews draws its words is found in Exodus 19:12-13, 17-21. The people *could not endure* the voice or the words the voice spoke. *The order that was given* was too much for them (Exodus 20:18-19; Deuteronomy 5:25). *Moses said, "I tremble with fear."* This may refer to Deuteronomy 9:19 where Moses fears *the anger and hot displeasure* of God.

Come to the Joyful City of God (12:22-24)

These verses describe, in contrast, the new mountain of God to which the Christians addressed in the sermon have come. *But you have come:* You are standing, as it were, before *Mount Zion*. The major hill in Jerusalem was and still is used as synonymous with Jerusalem, and is the symbolic center of Jewish faith. *To the city of the living God, the heavenly Jerusalem,* the city *whose builder and maker is God* (11:10). Unlike Mount Sinai where the people of the old covenant began their journey, Mount Zion is the city for which they were looking. *The heavenly Jerusalem* is the Jerusalem above, the true Jerusalem, city of God. Paul, the apostle, uses an allegory for a similar comparison between the old and new covenants in Galatians 4:21-26.

The true Jerusalem is the real sanctuary, in contrast with the earthly sanctuary, which was but a copy or shadow of the heavenly one (Hebrews 8–10). In contrast to the terrifying imagery of the old Sinai is the sublime scene in heaven. *To innumerable angels*: Heaven, according to popular Jewish literature, was the dwelling place of angels. The writer, however, probably had in mind the poem in Deuteronomy where *The LORD came from Sinai . . . from the ten thousands of holy ones* (Deuteronomy 33:2). *In festal gathering* is one word used in the Greek Old Testament for great exultant assemblies (as in Hosea 9:5).

Are angels meant? They have already been mentioned separately. Are they the Christians addressed? How, then, could they *come to . . . the assembly of the first-born* (verse 23)? They are *enrolled* (as citizens) *in heaven.* Paul (Philippians 4:3) and the Book of Revelation mention a "book of life" in which are enrolled the names of persons consecrated to Christ (see Revelation 21:27).

The writer to Hebrews is not striving for logical precision but simply presents a picture of the joyful experience in the heavenly Jerusalem. The *first-born* are those who are the first to have entered the new Jerusalem since Christ opened the way, and the faithful heroes of the past who have joined them (11:4; see also Revelation 6:9 and 1 Thessalonians 4:17). The "first-born" in Jewish law always belonged to God. They were consecrated to God. Israel, consecrated to God, was called God's first-born (Exodus 4:22). Christ is called the first-born in Hebrews 1:6, and by Paul in Colossians 1:18.

It is a mark of the supreme ruler (*a judge who is God of all,* verse 23) that he is judge of those he rules. God is judge of the universe at the last judgment. The element of reverence and awe is always evident in Hebrews' recognition of God. Apart from judgment there would be no meaning to righteousness and to grace (12:14-15). *The spirits of just men made perfect* are they who have lived just lives, approved for their faith (11:2). Now, being dead, their spirits are *made perfect,* that is, consecrated in God's presence by the sacrifice of Christ (11:39-40). Jesus, as *mediator of a new covenant,* has made all this possible for us. As the sprinkling of the sacrificed oxen's blood initiated the old covenant (Exodus 24:3-8), so the sprinkling of the blood of Christ, in his sacrifice of himself, initiated the new covenant. The popular interpretation of Abel's blood was that it was crying to the Lord (Genesis 4:10) for vengeance against Cain and his descendants. The victim calls for vengeance, the exclusion of the victimizer from God's mercy. Christ's blood *speaks more graciously*, on the other hand. It recalls Christ's prayer of forgiveness from the cross whereby the inclusion in God's grace is made available to all who will accept it.

Do Not Refuse God Who Calls You (12:25-27)

The author has just written about *the blood that speaks more graciously* (verse 24). This brings him to a last warning to those who *refuse him who is speaking*. This is the last contrast between what was spoken of and what God has spoken now through the Son (1:1-2), between the voice of the old covenant (verse 19) and the voice of the new covenant. If the first voice was terrifying to its hearers, the last voice is even more threatening to those who disparage it. Verses 25-27 contain a final warning not to throw away what God has offered us. It is a warning against turning back to the unstable, shakable religion of the law. For what God has now offered is unshakable. The glory of the new, or the heavenly, is greater than that of the old, earthly order of the old covenant. And, so much greater is the seriousness of rejecting it. This repeats the warning given in 2:2-3. The wonder of God speaking to us (1:1-2) suggests the enormity of our declining to hear. *They did not escape:* They who rebelled against the voice that spoke on earth died in the wilderness, never reaching the land of rest (3:17-19).

The old covenant was given through Moses on earth. The new covenant is given from heaven through Christ. Both were offers. Both are warnings, if rejected. The voice that spoke from Mount Sinai *shook the earth* (Exodus 19:18). The voice that speaks from heaven will shake the universe. Hebrews quotes this freely from Haggai 2:6, 21.

The writer takes (quoted directly from the Greek version of verse 6) the opening phrase of the promise *yet once more* to mean a final warning about the ending of the created universe, of *what has been made*. It is shakable, destructible. In the end only the unshakable new Jerusalem, not a part of the created universe, will remain.

Worship God With Thankfulness (12:28-29)

The writer again identifies with the Christians as he gives a positive conclusion to the warning.

Therefore carries on the emphasis of the previous sentence: *a kingdom that cannot be shaken*. The concept of *kingdom* (in the singular) is not used by Hebrews except in quotations from the Old Testament (1:8). It comes here from the quotation of the prophet Haggai about the overthrow of kingdoms. The old kingdoms will be shaken and overthrown. They are shadows. The true Kingdom, unshakable, will remain. The true Kingdom is what we are *receiving*: The tense of the participle is present. Also in the present is the experience of what Christ has already done for us. We will fully realize in the future what we begin to experience now.

Let us be grateful translates literally: *Let us have peace*. This fairly common Greek phrase for expressing thanks is our response to Christ's graciousness (12:24). Our awareness of God's grace leads us to *reverence and awe* in our gratitude for God's amazing gift of salvation. This is not an easy thanks made to an indulgent God. God's transcendent holiness makes the gift to us an undeserved wonder. It is divine grace that enables us to serve and worship God acceptably. *For* [let us never forget] *our God is a consuming fire*. This is a quotation from Deuteronomy 4:24 where the Israelites are reminded that God is *a jealous God*, a God who will not countenance any double-dealing in worship. No idolatry will be tolerated, no half-way consecration. God consumes all that is dross, or not genuine.

§ § § § § § §

The Message of Hebrews 12:18-29

In this passage the writer pictures the difference between the old covenant as Mount Sinai and the new covenant as Mount Zion. Characterizing the old as a religion of fear and the new as one of joy and fellowship with God's perfected people, the writer invites the Christians to receive the new covenant with gratitude and worship. In these verses Hebrews counsels us:

§ Do not settle for an earth-bound, legalistic religion; instead, join the company of those going on to the joyful fulfillment of God's promise in heaven—to God your judge and Jesus your savior.

§ Keep in mind that the things of this earth are unstable and will all come to an end.

§ Accept God's gift of forgiving grace with deep gratitude.

§ Worship God's absolute power, greatness, and judgment with awesome reverence.

§ § § § § § §

PART FIFTEEN Hebrews 13

Introduction to This Chapter

The sermon has ended. Chapter 13 is different, and perhaps does not belong with the rest of the book. Chapter 13 has two parts. The first part (verses 1-17) is Christian counsel. The second part closes the letter.

In the first section, each thought leads briefly into the next. Except for verses 11-14, however, which echo the emphases in the sermon, the counsel to Christians is abruptly different; it is direct and concise.

The second section closes the letter with a benediction in verse 21. Verses 22-25 are an added postscript.

Here is an outline of Hebrews 13.

I. Counsel for Christian Living (13:1-17)
   A. Care for those in need (13:1-3)
   B. Keep pure and free from greed (13:4-6)
   C. Trust in Christ (13:7-8)
   D. Live by God's grace (13:9-10)
   E. Join Jesus as an outcast (13:11-14)
   F. Praise God, witness, do good, share (13:15-16)
   G. Obey your leaders in the faith (13:17)
II. Closing of the Letter (13:18-21)
   A. Pray for us, pray for me (13:18-19)
   B. May Christ work in you (13:20-21)
III. Postscript (13:22-25)
   A. Heed this letter's counsel (13:22)
   B. Timothy and I may come soon (13:23)
   C. Greetings to your leaders (13:24)
   D. God's grace be with you (13:25)

Care for Those in Need (13:1-3)

Brotherly love holds the Christian congregation together and should be extended to those in special need. The word for *love* used here is not generally used in the New Testament for godly love for one another. Rather, it is the word commonly used in Greek for relations in a family. The Christians belong to the family in Christ. *Brotherly* is the inclusive word that ties all siblings together. *Let brotherly love continue.* It may be that these ties had become weakened among the Christians, as the sermon seems to suggest (10:24).

Hospitality to strangers (or friendship for strangers) was a long tradition in the Middle East, as frequently recorded in Old Testament stories. It was important among Christians in the urbanized world of the Roman Empire where there was much travel but few inns. *For thereby some have entertained angels unawares,* as did Abraham (Genesis 18) and Lot (Genesis 19). Apparently there was discussion among Christians as to how far this hospitality should go (see 2 John 10 and 3 John 5-8).

Remember those (fellow Christians) *who are in prison . . . and . . . ill-treated.* You are to sympathize with them as though you too were in chains (10:34). You too are in the body and you too could be imprisoned and ill-treated. It was because Christ was in the body that he could sympathize with us (2:18).

Keep Pure and Free From Greed (13:4-6)

Verse 4 is crystal clear. Because the influences of the sexually promiscuous society of the times could easily spill over into the church, this counsel was needed. Marriage was not and could not be held in honor where there was little honor attached to being a wife or a husband. Spouse-swapping, casual liaisons, and prostitution were quite common, and notoriously so both among civil leaders as well as in the vast slave population of the first century. One of the distinctions of the Jewish and Christian groups was the honorableness of the marriage state.

Immoral and *adulterous* are translations of two nouns. The first, which is the root word for *pornography*, refers to sexual promiscuity in general, and in particular to men who are unfaithful to their wives. The other word means the act of adultery with a married woman. Practices such as these defile the *marriage bed* and are condemned by God.

Love for family and love for strangers are positive loves. A love for money is negative. *Keep your life free from love of money*. Be satisfied with what is at hand.

Faithlessness to spouse and love for money are moral equivalents to drifting away from God. Trust in God. God does not fail you. In Deuteronomy 31:6-8 and Joshua 1:5 God assures the Israelites that they need not fear the enemy as they invade Canaan, for they will not be abandoned. The writer uses the same promise, applying it with a strengthened negative, God *will never fail you nor forsake you*, as an assurance of God's constant care of the Christians. There is no need to worry; God will provide (Matthew 6:25-34). In fact, we can be cheerful. The quotation is the old Greek version of Psalm 118:6.

Trust in Christ (13:7-8)

You have a good example in those who brought the faith to you. *Your leaders* are perhaps missionaries who brought the word of God to them. *Consider* the effect of their lives. *Outcome* is a word sometimes used for *conclusion* or *death*. In that case, then, these leaders, in loyalty to their faith, were martyred. In living or dying, their faith and faithfulness are an example to be followed.

Jesus Christ was the focus of their faith, the beginning and the perfecter of their faith (12:2), and he must be for all Christians now and forever. As James would say of God: *With whom there is no shadow . . . due to change* (James 1:17), so the writer says of Jesus. He, Christ, never changes, never abandons us.

Live by God's Grace (13:9-10)

Christians have been assured that God does not abandon them. Christ never changes. But they have been tempted to change, and to abandon Christ.

Do not be led away . . . In the Middle Eastern world in which Christianity first grew, there were many religions. Their shrines and temples, porches and gardens crowded each other. They offered a variety of beliefs and practices from philosophical discussions and mystical sophistries to secret ceremonies, orgies, and rituals. Many people moved easily from one religion to another or practiced more than one at the same time. Their ideas and practices influenced each other.

Some of these religions had even infiltrated into a few Jewish groups and tried to penetrate the Christian faith. Christian converts from paganism found some of the ideas and practices attractive. Paul had written to the Colossians about one in which food and drink regulations figured (Colossians 2:16-19). Some such teaching may have affected the Christian recipients of this letter, for it speaks of *foods, which have not benefited their adherents*. God's grace nourishes our hearts and minds. Nothing we eat will strengthen us from the weakness of sin in our lives, only the *grace* of God in Jesus Christ.

Speaking of food leads the writer to the subject of food offered on religious altars. In some religions a food, having been offered on the altar to the god, was distributed among worshipers as a symbol of their participation in the energy of the god. Christians did not share in such food.

It may be that the problem of the Christians was not the influence of another religion but the tendency simply to slip into religious practices of Judaism which had food regulations to which it held strictly. The writer returns to the difference discussed in the sermon between the earthly Levitical sanctuary sacrifices, and the heavenly. There was an altar in the center of the court of the tent of meeting described in Exodus 27:1-8. It was the altar of the old covenant. *We* [Christians] *have an altar* [of the new covenant] *from which those who serve the tent have no right to eat.* Rather, they have no capacity to eat from this altar because they have not accepted the sacrifice, that of Christ, which it represents. Their food, by Mosaic law, is the food that is offered at the altar in the earthly sanctuary. They have no place among us. Some commentators have wondered about the phrase *we have an altar.* Was the writer thinking of either the cross, on which Christ sacrificed himself, or the Communion table? He is speaking figuratively, as in the sermon, of the heavenly altar of Christ's self-sacrifice which is the center of Christian worship.

Join Jesus as an Outcast (13:11-14)

Mention of the animal sacrifices from the altar in the earthly tent of meeting leads the writer to another word about faithfulness to Jesus. According to Jewish law (Leviticus 16:27), only the blood of the sin-offering on the Day of Atonement was carried by the high priest into the Holy of Holies in the sanctuary. The carcasses of the animals sacrificed were taken out and *burned outside the camp* of the wandering Israelites. Jesus, the ultimate sacrifice, was crucified outside the Jerusalem city gate. His body was outside the camp, but his blood was offered at the true, heavenly sanctuary and has consecrated his people. The writer may have known of a party of Jews called the Essenes who considered that the Temple, the actual priesthood, and Judaism in general had become contaminated and impure. They felt that they, the Essenes, were the true Israel; others were just a copy. So they went "outside the gate" where they were following a more disciplined life and where the messiah, they said, would come to them.

On the basis of these illustrations, the writer counsels: You cannot compromise, belonging partly to the old order and partly to the new. Since Jesus is so incomparably superior as the real access to God, join him *outside the camp*, bearing abuse for him. Jesus was abused with insult and injury. Christians who cling to him must be ready to bear his disgrace, because they have moved out of this earthly city.

The earthly Jerusalem, like the old covenant, is not the real "city of God." It is not lasting. The writer asks that we, like pilgrims of faith, move out and seek a better city, the city which is to come (Matthew 6:33).

Praise God, Witness, Do Good, Share (13:15-16)

As God's grace is more nourishing to the heart than ritual food, as Christ is more effective for salvation than animal sacrifices, so our sacrifice of *the fruit of lips that acknowledge his name* is better than the formal offering in the old covenant sanctuary.

Christ made the ultimate sacrifice, once for all in our behalf. But we, too, can offer up a sacrifice continually *through him* who is our high priest (9:15). Our sacrifice will be our *praise to God*, made openly to direct attention to God, to acknowledge God's name, *for it is good* (Psalm 54:6). A life directed in praise to God is *to do good and to share* with others a *sacrifice acceptable and pleasing to God* (Philippians 4:18).

Obey Your Leaders in the Faith (13:17)

You have leaders in the faith whose concern is your spiritual well-being. News of problems in the Christian group, such as their loss of dedication (10:32-36) or slackness in personal living (13:4-5) or attraction to *strange teachings* (verse 9) may have come to the writer from the leaders. They are deeply concerned about the Christians they lead. *They* (emphatic) *watch over* them like parents losing sleep to care for their family. They feel accountable to God for the people they have in charge. Such care would be a joy if they were leading a joyful, enthusiastic group of Christians. A careless, indifferent group makes their watch-care a sad one, one that literally causes groaning. That does the Christian group no good.

Therefore, the writer urges the people: *Obey* your spiritual leaders and *submit* to their guidance, for they are the ones who lead you in the faith. The word translated *obey* has many meanings, such as *to listen, to assent, to trust,* or *to follow*. All of these meanings are what the writer is asking the Christians to do. It is an appeal to be responsive to wise and loving care. The advice to *submit* suggests that they have been unresponsive, even obstinate.

Pray for Us, Pray for Me (13:18-19)

In closing the letter, the writer asks the readers to pray for him. They know who he is, but no identifying signature has come in the letter. *Pray for us* or, precisely, *continue to pray for us*. The *us* is a formal request with which Paul often closed his letters. *For we are sure*: There must have been some criticism, some questioning of the motives of the writer. Nevertheless, his conscience is clear and his intentions are to do what is right. Verse 19 adds an appeal: *I urge you the more earnestly,* or particularly urge you. All the more I beseech you to do this: to keep on praying, *that I* [a more personal request] *may be restored to you the sooner*. Was he waiting to be sure of acceptance with them? We can only guess.

May Christ Work in You (13:20-21)

The benediction closes the letter. It is a heartfelt wish for blessings on the Christians and a confident trust in God's power. The doxology at the end, *to whom be glory,* is typical of first-century Christian letters to congregations. The blessing wish is that the same power of God who raised Jesus equip you for God's work and work through us.

God is the *God of peace* (verse 20). Peace encompasses salvation. This verse has the one explicit reference to the

Resurrection in Hebrews. In previous passages, Jesus has pierced the veil to present his blood in the heavenly Holy of Holies, thus initiating the new covenant. Here it is God's action. It was *God who has spoken to us by a Son* in the opening sentence (1:2). Now, in the last sentence, it is God *who brought again from the dead our Lord Jesus*. God in the beginning! God is the ending! Through Christ, sent into the world, God has spoken. Through Christ, brought again from the world, God saves us.

The imagery changes. Jesus, who has been depicted as the high priest offering the supreme sacrifice, himself, is here the *great shepherd* caring for his sheep. Christians who have accepted the new covenant are his sheep. The figure was one used frequently of the Lord and the people in Old Testament passages: *He will feed his flock like a shepherd, he will gather the lambs in his arms* (Isaiah 40:11).

God *equip you* to *do his will*. *Equip* suits the sermon's thesis that Christ perfects us, for *equip* means to qualify something by adjusting, repairing, and refitting. May God work *in you that which is pleasing in his sight* and is synonymous with *his will*. Most manuscripts have *in us*, not *in you*. If *in us*, the writer is identifying with them as Christ's sheep.

A postscript is added to the letter, either by the writer or by someone else who is sending it. Similar postscripts are attached to 2 Timothy (4:19-20), Philippians (4:21-23), and 1 Peter (5:12-14).

Heed This Letter's Counsel (13:22)

Bear with my advice. The uncertainty recurs as to how the readers will react to the sermon-letter (see the comments on verses 18-19). I do hope you will put up with *my word of exhortation*. I urge you to do so.

I have written to you briefly. This could apply to the entire sermon, or to the letter which is attached (Chapter 13), as though the author were saying, "Enclosed please find . . ." Briefly? Nevertheless, the author had already expressed the feeling that the message, although it may seem long to us (an hour's sermon), was too brief to say all that could be said (5:11; 9:5; 11:32).

Timothy and I May Come Soon (13:23)

Timothy has been released. This implies that Timothy had been in prison. Timothy is often mentioned in Acts and in Paul's letters as Paul's traveling companion and emissary (Acts 19:22). If the author added this postscript, it is a hope (verse 19) for an early meeting, together with Timothy, with the Christians to whom the sermon is sent.

Greetings to Your Leaders (13:24)

The recipients of the letter have been advised to *remember your leaders* (verse 7), although the reference may be to former leaders, and to *obey your leaders* (verse 17). Now they are told to *greet all your leaders*. The Christians are receiving the letter apart from, or with, their leaders. They may be a house group too far apart to meet with all the Christians and their leaders except at intervals. Or they may be a group that has drifted away from their leaders (10:24-25).

All the saints are the Christians. Saints (holy ones) was a common designation for Christians as a group who were bound together by the Holy Spirit (see comment on 6:10).

Who were the Italians? *Those . . . from Italy* sounds, as the Revised Standard Version translates it, as though they *come from Italy*. Is the church receiving the letter in Italy and being greeted by fellow Italian Christians? Or is the writer in Italy and sending greetings from an Italian Christian church? Either translation is possible.

God's Grace Be With You (13:25)

The word *greetings* that ended most letters of the time was turned into *grace* by Christians. Christians live by grace, and by grace they are related to one another.

§ § § § § § §

The Message of Hebrews 13

This chapter is a pastoral letter, distinct from, but related to, the sermon that preceded it. It is a letter of counsel to Christians. It includes moral advice about the Christians' relationship to the new covenant with God through Christ. It closes with a request for prayer, a benediction, a doxology, and a postscript. It tells us:

§ to care for one another in the Christian fellowship;
§ to show hospitality to strangers;
§ to extend our caring to all who are in trouble, in prison, or abused for their faith;
§ to do all the good we can, sharing what we have;
§ to keep marriage sacred, avoiding all extra-marital sexual relations;
§ to be always aware of God's judgment against sexual promiscuity and adultery;
§ to live a life free of love of money; to abhor greed;
§ to be content with what we have, trusting in God to provide what we need;
§ to maintain the serenity of those who know Christ is ever the same and will never change;
§ to imitate the faith of Christian leaders, follow their advice, and pray for them;
§ to avoid cults, religious fads, and tabus;
§ not to mind belonging to a faith that is different from the patterns of worldly belief and behavior;
§ to accept abuse for Christ's sake who, himself, was discarded by society;
§ to keep in mind the transience of the things of this world, the enduring reality of Christ;
§ to praise God daily, openly, and to glorify Christ;
§ to live by and share God's grace.

§ § § § § § §

Glossary of Terms

Aaron: Brother of Moses, Israel's leader. Aaron was designated as high priest to lead Israel's worship of God. His descendants were to be Israel's priests.
Aaron's rod: The rod, representing the tribe of Levi, budded as a proof of God's will that they should be the priests of Israel.
Abel: The second son of Adam and Eve. His sacrifice was pleasing to God. Because of this, his brother, Cain, killed him.
Abraham: Ancestor of all Jews. A man of strong faith in God. His name means *father of a multitude*.
Age, ages, age to come: There are two ages: the *present* age of the created universe in which we live, and *the age to come*, initiated by Jesus' incarnation, and consummated on his return. Hebrews says that the age to come will supersede the present age.
Angels: Ministering spirits created by God to help those who are to obtain salvation.
Apostasy: Leaving the Christian fellowship; deliberately turning away from Christ and the Christian faith, and God's offer of salvation.
Ark of the covenant: An oblong box overlaid with gold, kept in the Most Holy Place in the sanctuary of Israel. In it were kept the tablets engraved with the Ten Commandments.
Barak: Along with Deborah, a leader in the confederacy of Israelite tribes.
Blood: Because blood is life, the sacrificed blood in a religious ritual is considered to have a cleansing power. Symbolically, the blood of Jesus, sacrificed in behalf of humanity, has the

power to cleanse the conscience of those who accept Christ as savior.

Bread of the Presence: Bread placed fresh every week on a table by the curtain that separated God's "presence" in the Holy of Holies from the rest of the sanctuary.

Cain: The oldest son of Adam and Eve. His sacrifice was less pleasing to God than his brother Abel's. Therefore, he killed Abel.

Cherubim of glory: Two images of symbolic winged creatures guarding the mercy seat which covered the ark of the covenant.

Christ: The Greek translation of Messiah, the anointed one of God. This was the title affixed by Christians to Jesus, the Christ.

Covenant: An agreement. God, through grace, offered to an undeserving but chosen people a special relationship as their guide and protector. The people, for their part, willingly bound themselves to faithful obedience to God's law. Because the people repeatedly broke their part of the covenant, the prophet Jeremiah promised that God would give them a new covenant written indelibly on their conscience. This new covenant of the spirit is mediated through Jesus Christ.

David: Early heroic king of Israel. Known as the writer of many of the psalms.

Day (of the Lord): The time of the return of Christ and the ending of the present age; the day of judgment and the age to come.

Day of Atonement: The once-a-year high holy day when the high priest of Israel, having made sacrifices for his own sins and those of his household, and of all the priests, took the blood of sacrificed animals into the Most Holy Place. He sprinkled the blood on the mercy seat and on the floor in front as a expression of the people's repentance for sins, and a reconciliation with God.

Destroyer: The Angel of Death who brought about the death of all first-born in Egypt, with the exception of those in Israelite homes.

Doctrines: Teachings; instructions.

Egypt: Ancient country in the northeast corner of Africa. Here the Israelites were held in slavery until led by Moses across the desert northeast toward Canaan.

Endurance: Bearing hardships and difficulties patiently as disciplines from God; the quality of those who are faithful to God.

Enoch: Ancient hero of dedicated faith. He was taken up to be with God without having to die.

Esau: Elder son of Isaac. Brother of Jacob.

Eternal: That which pertains to the age to come after the present age. It will be forever.

Faith, faithfulness: Action based on confidence in and loyalty to Christ. A life directed perseveringly toward God and God's will for humankind.

Gideon: A leader in the confederacy of Israelite tribes.

Grace, God's grace, Spirit of Grace: God's enabling human creatures, through the incarnation and suffering of the Son, to be cleansed of sin and so have access to God.

Heaven, heavens: (1) Created space above the earth. (2) Uncreated, eternal place of God.

Holiness: The awesome perfection and absolute righteousness of God. Purity and righteousness of those who belong to God.

Holy of Holies (the Most Holy Place): Smaller of the two rooms in the sanctuary of Israel, curtained off at its west end. Shaped like a cube. Restricted to entry by the high priest and then only once a year on the Day of Atonement. Here was kept the ark of the covenant.

Holy Place: The larger of the two rooms in the sanctuary of Israel. Rectangular in shape. Restricted to serving priests. Furnished with a table of the bread of Presence, a seven-branched lampstand, and altar of incense.

Holy Spirit: God's Spirit, which (1) speaks through the Scriptures, (2) expresses God's grace, (3) distributes abilities to believers, and (4) through whom Christ offers himself, and (5) with whom Christians share fellowship.

Hope: Confident expectation of access to God, such that it affects one's life direction.

House: (1) God's people (Israel, Christians); (2) the sanctuary built by Moses for worship; (3) the heavenly sanctuary where God is.
Isaac: Son of Abraham, ancestor of Israel.
Israel: The people led by Moses out of slavery in Egypt. Members of the twelve tribes descended from Jacob (Israel). People of God's covenant.
Israelites: The people of Israel.
Jacob: Son of Isaac, grandson of Abraham. Father of the twelve tribes of Israel.
Jephthah: A leader in the confederacy of Israelite tribes.
Jericho: Ancient city near the Dead Sea west of the Jordan River. The first city attacked by the Israelites as they invaded Canaan.
Joshua: Successor to Moses who led the people of Israel into the land God promised them (Canaan).
Judah: The fourth son of Israel's ancestor, Jacob. The tribe of Judah from which were descended the kings.
Judgment: Follows after death. God is the ultimate judge. Judgment condemns to eternal separation from God those who have neglected salvation and preferred unrighteousness.
Law: Commandments given by God to Israel through Moses. The Ten Commandments. Laws detailed in Exodus through Deuteronomy.
Levi: The third son of Israel's ancestor, Jacob, great-grandson of Abraham. His descendants were designated priests and priest-assistants in Israel.
Levites: People of the tribe of Levi.
Levitical: Pertaining to the priesthood of Israel, descendants of Levi, and the laws and ceremonies they administered.
Manna: Food supplied by God to the hungry Israelites in their desert crossing.
Melchizedek: "Prince of Righteousness," priest-king of Salem. He blessed Abram. His priesthood is greater than Aaron's.
Mercy Seat: Gold slab covering the ark of the covenant in the Holy of Holies. The sanctuary of Israel. It represented the

place of God's presence to meet the high priest on the Day of Atonement.

Messiah: Anointed one. The Messiah is anointed by God to fulfill the divine promises in the end times, that is, on the Day of the Lord.

Moses: Leader of Israel in its escape from slavery in Egypt. He instituted the covenant with God, built the tent of meeting according to a pattern God gave him, and delivered God's law to Israel.

Mount Zion: The major hill in Jerusalem, symbolic of Jerusalem; also symbolic of the city of God.

Noah: Patriarch who, at God's command, built an ark in which he saved his family from the flood.

Oil of Gladness: Oil poured on the head of a king at his coronation. Signified an occasion of celebration, joy, and gladness.

Passover: The Angel of Death which passed over and spared the homes of the Israelites who had sprinkled the blood of a lamb on their doorposts and lintels. In all other homes the firstborn died.

Patriarch: An ancestor in ancient Israel. Especially applied to the earthly heroic ancestors of the Jews, primarily Abraham, Isaac, and Jacob.

Perfection: Consecration to God. Made acceptable to God. Arrival at the place where, cleansed of sin, the faithful are acceptable in the presence of God.

Pharaoh: Title of the ruler of ancient Egypt. Also called the king of Egypt.

Presence: The presence of God in the Holy of Holies in the sanctuary of Israel and in the heavens.

Promise: God's promise to (1) Abraham that his descendants would be a great nation; (2) Israel that they would be guided to a land of rest in rich Canaan; (3) faithful Christians that, through Christ, they will reach eternal rest with God.

Purification: (1) A priestly act that pronounces a worshiper purified of sin on the basis of a sacrifice made. (2) The result of Jesus' self-sacrifice whereby a sinner is made acceptable to

enter the presence of God.
Rahab: A prostitute in Jericho who protected and saved the lives of Israel's spies.
Red Sea: The body of water that divides Egypt from Arabia. Escaping from Egypt, the Israelites crossed it.
Rest: (1) The land promised to the desert-wandering Israelites. (2) The eternal experience of the presence of God, enabled by Christ.
Righteousness: Rectitude. The opposite of lawlessness. Adhering to God's law. Justice. Doing right to all in obedience to God, who is righteous and just. Justice includes anger and judgment against sin and, at the same time, the way of salvation and reconciliation with God.
Root of Bitterness: A symbolic root bearing bitter or poisonous fruit that causes people to sin and thus to turn away from God.
Sacrifice: (1) The ritual killing of an animal as a means of restoring broken relationships with God. (2) The supreme sacrifice of Christ so that all might have access to God.
Salem: An ancient city of which Melchizedek was king at the time of Abraham. Another name for Jerusalem. It means *peace.*
Salvation: Freed from sin, arrived in the presence of God, there to rest forever. Wholeness in fellowship with Christ and God.
Samson: A leader in the confederacy of Israelite tribes who single-handedly protected Israel from foreign oppressors.
Samuel: The last political leader in the Israelite confederacy who, as a prophet, selected and ordained Israel's first kings, Saul and David.
Sanctified: Made holy. Consecrated to God.
Sarah: Wife of Abraham, mother of Isaac, ancestor of the Israelite people.
Sin: Disobedience to God's law. Whatever separates us from God, such as neglecting to live by faith, indifference to God's grace, immorality.
Son (of God): A term used to signify the uniquely close eternal

relationship of Christ with God; it is a title of the reflection of Christ to God.

Soul: The totality of a human life. According to Hebrews, the soul is the spiritual existence of humankind before God. It lives by means of hope in the future, where God invites it to live in God's presence forever.

Spirit: (see *Holy Spirit*)

Suffering: (1) Christ's suffering involved in his breaking the barrier of human separation from God. (2) Human suffering occasioned in humankind's faithful movement through this world to God.

Tables of the Covenant: Stone tablets on which were engraved the Ten Commandments.

Tent of meeting: A portable sanctuary; it was the center of worship for the people of Israel during their desert wanderings.

Timothy: A friend of the writer of Hebrews and of the people to whom the author wrote. Probably the same as Paul's friend.

Word of God: (1) The Bible (Old Testament). (2) The action of God. (3) Christ as God's communication to human beings. (4) Christ as God's agent of creation.

Guide to Pronunciation

Aaron: AIR-un
Abel: AY-bel
Abraham: AY-brah-ham
Apostasy: Ah-POS-teh-see
Barak: Bah-RACK
Cherubim: CHAIR-uh-bim
Enoch: EE-nuk
Esau: EE-saw
Gideon: GID-ee-un
Isaac: EYE-zek
Jephthah: JEF-thah
Jericho: JEH-rih-koh
Joshua: JOSH-oo-ah
Judah: JOO-dah
Levi: LEE-vigh
Levites: LEE-vites
Levitical: Leh-VIH-tih-kal
Manna: MAN-nah
Melchizedek: Mel-KIH-zih-deck
Messiah: Meh-SIGH-ah
Noah: NOH-ah
Pharaoh: FAY-roh
Rahab: RAY-hab
Salem: SAY-lem
Samuel: SAM-yoo-ell
Samson: SAM-son
Sarah: SEHR-ah
Timothy: TIH-moh-thee

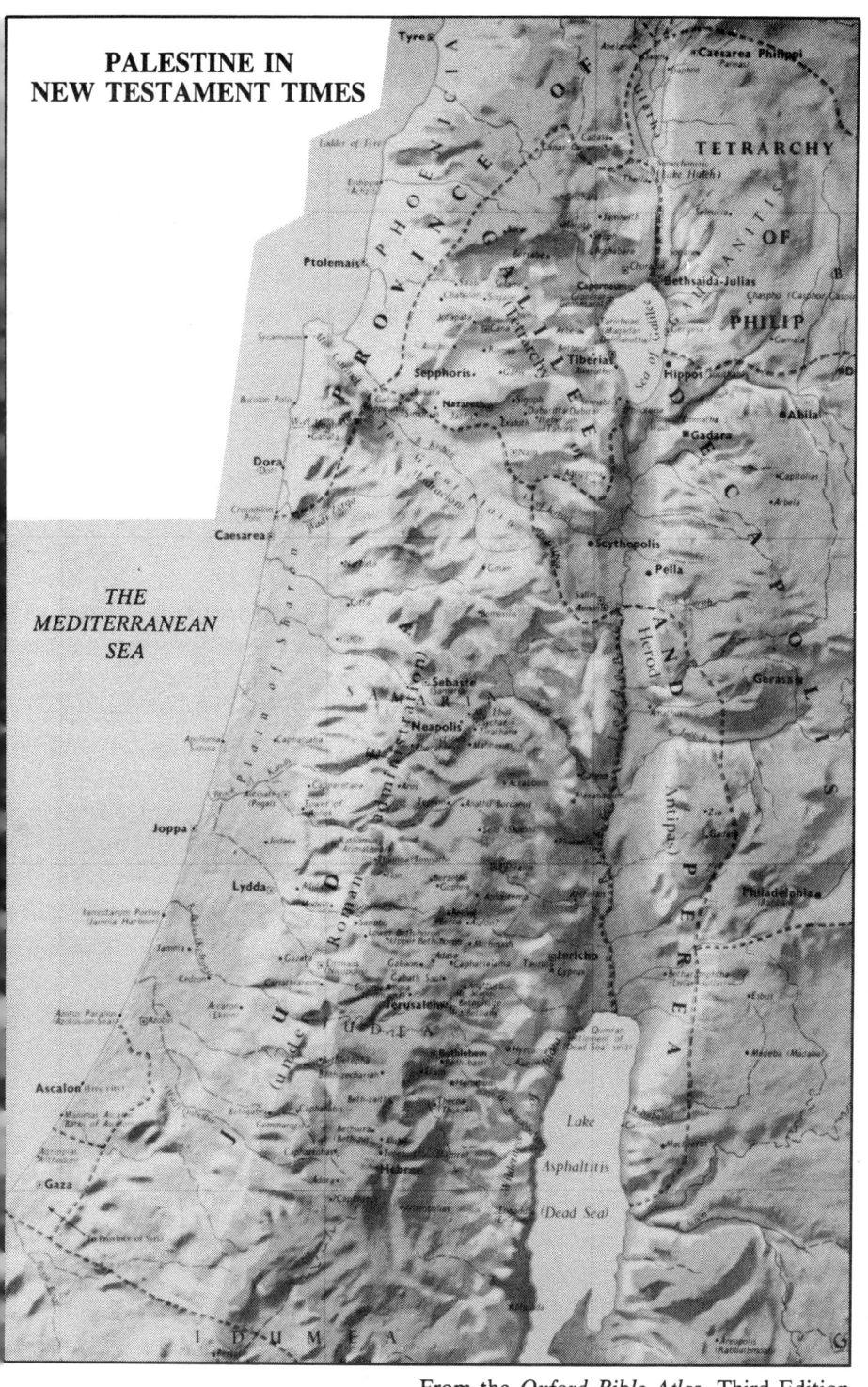

From the *Oxford Bible Atlas*, Third Edition